FOREX TRADING FOR BEGINNERS

By

Alex Kim

TABLE OF CONTENTS

INTRODUCTION

If you've ever traveled abroad, you've been engaged in the world of currency exchange, though you may not know: when you got off the plane, one of your first stops was probably switching your money to the local currency.

Currency trading transforms this small airport or ATM exchange into a forex trading outlet. When investors trade foreign exchange, commonly known as FX, they buy and sell currencies in the forex market. It is the largest financial market in the world, but many individual investors have never tried trading in it, in part because it is highly speculative and complex.

A sound approach serves investors well. Active trading strategies and complex investment products are unmatched in most portfolios. Low index funds are strongly recommended for long-term purposes, such as retirement savings.

But maybe he is financially stable, and now he's looking for an adventure with a little more money. While you know what you are doing, take these steps seriously, so that currency trading can be lucrative and requires limited initial investment.

Differentiating currency trading and stock trading

Exchange transactions are negotiated between traders or operators in foreign currencies, rather than through a central exchange. Because the trader works in many time zones, the forex market is open 24 hours a day, five days a week. The currencies are always traded in pairs, and prices are quoted in pairs.

Currency prices fluctuate rapidly but in small increments, preventing investors from earning money on smaller transactions. This is why currencies are almost always traded with leverage or money provided by the broker.

Since the currencies are mentioned in pairs, they always exchange one currency for another, buy one and sell the other, as you would in a currency exchange kiosk. There are seven so-called "major" currencies, or more common: the euro (EUR), the US dollar (USD), the Canadian dollar (CAD), the British pound (GBP), the Australian dollar (AUD), the Japanese yen (JPY) and the Swiss franc (CHF). The "main pairs" are those currencies with the US dollar.

WHAT IS THE FOREX MARKET?

The forex market is where the currencies are traded. Currencies are essential for most people in the world, whether they realize it or not because they must be exchanged for commercial and business-related purposes abroad. If you live in the United States and want to buy cheese from France, you or the company from which you buy cheese must pay for French cheese in euros (EUR). This means that the US importer must exchange the equivalent in US dollars (USD) in euros. The same goes for traveling. A French tourist in Egypt cannot pay in euros to see the pyramids because it is not the locally accepted currency. However, the tourist will have to exchange euros for the local currency, in this case, the Egyptian pound, at the current exchange rate.

A unique aspect of this international market is that there is no central market for currencies. Currency trading is done electronically, which means that all transactions are done by computer networks between operators around the world rather than in a single centralized exchange. The market is open 24 hours a day, five days a week, and the currency is traded worldwide in major financial centers, namely London, New York, Tokyo, Zurich, Frankfurt, Hong Kong, Singapore, Paris, and Sydney – every time slot. This means that when the trading day ends in the US, the currency market is reborn in Tokyo and Hong Kong.

However, the currency market can be extremely active at any time of the day, with prices constantly changing.

HISTORY OF FOREX TRADING

The origin of forex trading traces its history centuries ago. Different currencies and the need to exchange them have existed since the Babylonians. There are artifacts with the first use of tickets and paper receipts. Speculation has never been made, and the immense speculative activity in the market has been tackled.

At the time, the value of the goods was expressed in terms of other goods (also called the barter system). The apparent limitations of such a system led to the more generally accepted means of exchange. It was important that a common value base could be established. In some economies, materials such as teeth, feathers, and even stones have been used for this purpose. Still, many metals, including gold and silver, have been established as an acceptable means of payment and a source of value. Therefore, reliable trade was made between the people of Africa, Asia, etc. through this system.

The currencies were initially stamped from the preferred metal and under stable political regimes, the introduction of a printed form of the I.O.U. In the Middle Ages, it also earned acceptance. This type of I.O.U. was introduced more effectively by force than by persuasion and is now the basis of modern currencies.

Before World War I, most central banks had taken their currencies with gold convertibility. However, the gold trading standard has its weaknesses in terms of expansion and deceleration of structures. As your economy strengthens, it will matter a lot from the outside until your gold reserves are depleted to manage your money; as a result, the money supply decreases, interest rates rise, and economic activity slows to the point of a recession. In the end, commodity prices have skyrocketed, apparently appealing to other countries, who are reluctant to buy the gold-fueled rage in the economy to increase their money supply, reducing interest rates. In exchange for gold, central banks do not necessarily need full coverage of government currency reserves. It doesn't happen very often. However, when a group espoused this disastrous notion of massive conversion into gold, panic gave birth to what is called "Run on Banks." The combination of a larger supply of paper without gold to cover led to devastating inflation and political instability. The Great Depression and the abolition of the gold standard in 1931 resulted in a severe pause in forex trading activity. From 1931 to 1973, the forex market underwent a series of changes. These changes greatly affected the world economy at that time, and speculation in currency markets during this period was weak. To protect local, national interests, more exchange controls have been implemented to prevent market forces from punishing monetary responsibility.

Towards the end of World War II, the Bretton Woods agreement was concluded at the initiative of the United States in July 1944. The conference arranged in Bretton Woods, New Hampshire, rejected John Maynard Keynes' proposal to create a new Global Reserve currency for a built system. In the US dollar, international institutions such as the IMF, the World Bank, and the GATT have been created in time, since the emerging victors of World War II have been looking for a way to avert the destabilizing monetary crisis leading to the war. The Bretton Woods deal resulted in a fixed exchange system that partially restored The Gold Standard, set the USD at $ 35.00 per ounce of gold, and set the other major currencies in the US dollar, initially earmarked for being permanent.

The Bretton Woods system was under increasing pressure as national economies moved in different directions during the 1960s. Several realignments kept the system alive for a long time, but Bretton Woods finally collapsed in the early 1970s, after the suspension of President Nixon's gold convertibility in August 1971. It was no longer the only international currency at this time.

Over the past few decades, trading has become the largest market in the world. Restrictions on capital flows have been eliminated in most countries, leaving free market forces to adjust exchange rates according to their perceived values. The European Economic Community established a new fixed exchange system in 1979, the European Monetary System. The search for monetary stability in Europe continued with the signing of the Maastricht Treaty in 1991. This was aimed not only at setting exchange rates, but also at replacing many of those with the euro in 2002. London was and continues to be the main offshore market. In the 1980s, it became the nerve center of the Eurodollar market when British banks began lending dollars instead of pounds to maintain their leading position in world finance.

In Asia, the lack of sustainability of fixed exchange rates became more relevant to events in Southeast Asia at the end of 1997, where currency after currency was devalued relative to the US dollar, leaving other rates fixed exchange rates, especially in southern countries.

While trading companies have had to deal with a much more volatile monetary environment in recent years, investors and financial institutions have discovered a new playing field. The foreign currency market initially operated by central banks and government institutions, then was the host of different institutions. Currently, it also includes the booms of e-commerce and the world wide web. The weight of the forex market now exceeds any other investment market. The forex market is the largest financial market in the world. About $ 1.9 trillion is traded daily in this market. You can easily say that the forex market is a lucrative opportunity for the modern investor.

CURRENCIES TRADED ON FOREX MARKET

Six Most Popular Currencies for Trading

The currency market (or exchange) is the largest and most liquid market in the world, with billions of dollars exchanged daily between millions of parties. For those new to the forex market, one of the first steps is to familiarize yourself with some of the most common currencies and their popular uses in the forex market, but also in general. Here is a summary of six popular currencies with which all currency observers should be informed, in addition to the features and underlying characteristics of each currency.

1. The US dollar

Firstly, the US dollar, which is easily the most traded currency on the planet. The USD is in conjunction with all other major currencies and often serves as an intermediary in triangular currency transactions. In fact, the US dollar is the unofficial global reserve currency of almost all banks and institutional investment entities in the world.

In addition, due to the global acceptance of the US dollar, some countries use it as the official currency, instead of the local currency, a practice known as dollarization. The US dollar can also be widely accepted in other countries, acting as another form of informal payment, while these countries retain their official local currency.

The US dollar is also an important influence in the foreign exchange market, where it can serve as a benchmark or target tax for countries that choose to establish or link their currency with the value of the US dollar. China, for example, has already had its currency, the yuan or the renminbi, tied to the dollar, sharply in contrast to many central economists and bankers. Often, countries have imposed their USD exchange to stabilize their trade instead of letting the free (forex) markets fluctuate their relative value.

Forex beginners should understand that another feature of the

USD is that it is used as the standard currency for most trades, such as crude oil and precious metals. Therefore, these products are subject not only to fluctuations in value due to the economic fundamentals of supply and demand while at the same time to the relative value of the US dollar, with prices highly sensitive to inflation, rates of growth, and US interests, which directly affect the value of the dollar.

2. The euro

Although relatively new on the world stage, the euro has become the second most traded currency after the US dollar. The euro is also the second-largest reserve currency in the world. The official currency of most countries in the eurozone, the euro, was introduced on world markets on January 1, 1999, after which banks and currencies were put into circulation three years later.

In addition to being the official currency of most euro area countries, many countries in Europe and Africa link their currencies with the euro, for the same reason that currencies are indexed to the USD to stabilize the exchange.

As the euro is a widely used and reliable currency, it is commonly used in the currency market and adds liquidity to all currency pairs in which it trades. Speculators generally negotiated that the euro plays with the health of the eurozone and its members in general. Political events in the euro area can often bring large volumes of trade for the euro, especially against countries that have seen their local interest rates decline sharply at the time of creation. The euro is especially used in Italy, Greece, Spain, and Portugal. It is perhaps the most "politicized" currency in the currency market.

3. The Japanese yen

The Japanese yen is by far the most traded currency outside of Asia and seen by many as an indicator of the fundamental strength of Japan's manufacturing economy. Like a Japanese economy, the yen (in some ways) disappears. Many use the yen to assess the overall health of the Pacific region, including economies such as South Korea, Singapore, and Thailand, as these currencies are traded far less in global currency markets.

The yen is also known in monetary circles for its role in the transport trade (which seeks to take advantage of the difference in interest rates between two currencies). Japan has been following a zero interest rate policy for over two decades, and traders have taken the yen at virtually zero cost and have used it to invest in other high yielding currencies around the world, accumulating differential rates. Portage is an important part of the yen's presence on the international scene, and the constant lending of the Japanese currency has made it difficult to appreciate the currency. Even if the yen is trading in the same fund as any other currency, its relationship with international interest rates, especially with the most cited currencies, such as the US dollar and the euro, is a determining factor in the value of the yen.

4. The British Pound

The British pound sterling, also known as the British pound, is the fourth most traded currency in the currency market. It is also a large reserve of money because of its relative value compared to other world currencies. Although the United Kingdom is still an official member of the European Union, it has chosen not to use the euro as its official currency for a variety of reasons, including the historical pride of the pound and the continued control of taxes or interest. For this reason, the pound can be considered a pure game in the UK. Forex traders often base their value on the overall strength of the UK economy and the political stability of their government. Because of its high value relative to its peers, the pound is also a benchmark. It is an important currency for many countries and is a very liquid component in the currency market.

5. The Canadian dollar

More commonly known as the loonie, the Canadian dollar is possibly the most important production currency in the world, which means it keeps pace with commodity markets, including crude oil, precious metals, and minerals. As Canada is a major exporter of these products, the Canadian dollar is highly volatile against fluctuations in its underlying prices, especially crude oil prices. Merchants often trade the Canadian dollar to speculate on the movements of these commodities or to protect themselves from these possibilities in these underlying contracts.

In addition, the proximity of the largest consumer base in the world, the United States, to the Canadian economy and, therefore, to the Canadian dollar, is strongly correlated with the strength of the US economy and fluctuations of the US dollar.

6. The Swiss franc

The last one is the Swiss franc, which, like Switzerland, is considered by many to be a "neutral" currency. More specifically, the Swiss franc is considered a safe haven in the currency market, mainly because the franc have a tendency to to move in a negative correlation with more volatile commodity currencies, such as the Canadian dollar and the US dollar. In fact, we know that the Swiss National Bank is very active in the currency market to ensure that the franc is traded in a relatively tight range, to reduce volatility and keep interest rates under control.

MINOR AND EXOTIC CURRENCIES

Minors

Australian Dollar/AUD/A $

New Zealand Dollar/NZD/NZ $

Canada Dollar/CAD/C $

Exotic currencies

There are many other countries in the world, and most of them have their own currency. In addition to the major and secondary currencies, there is an important group of "exotic currencies."

Exotic currencies are made up of hundreds of currencies that are not included in major or minor leagues, but which are important, especially in international trade and finance.

Exotic includes:

RUB - the red ruble

CNY - the Chinese yuan or renminbi

BRL - the Brazilian royal

MXN - The Mexican peso

CLP - the Chilean peso

INR - the Indian rupee

TIR - the Iranian rial

These are just some of the most actively traded exotic currencies. In some cases, a country will use the US dollar as its currency, for example, a country like Haiti.

The Chinese yuan

An exotic currency that is rarely seen in the currency market is the Chinese yuan or renminbi. The reason is that the yuan is pegged to the US dollar, and the exchange that the Chinese hold when intervening in the currency market is currently fixed at 8,277 yuan per dollar.

This means that every time the US dollar moves, the Chinese

yuan moves with it. In other words, if the dollar grows against the euro, the yuan will increase against the euro by about the same percentage.

Currently, the Chinese artificially keep the yuan at a low level against the US dollar. This benefits the Chinese industry since it artificially maintains China's wage in US dollars, which makes China-made products extremely competitive in the global market.

WHAT IS CURRENCY PAIRS?

Currency pairs are the national currencies of two partner countries to operate in the currency market (FX). Both currencies have exchange rates on which the trade will have its basis of position. All currency market exchanges, whether sold, traded, or exchanged, will be made in pairs.

Generally speaking, the eight most traded currencies (in no particular order) are the US dollar (USD), the British pound (GBP), the Canadian dollar (CAD), the New Zealand dollar (NZD), the euro (EUR), the Swiss franc (CHF), the Australian dollar (AUD) and the Japanese yen (JPY).

Almost all countries' currencies can be traded, but some currencies are closer to other currencies. All major currency pairs contain USD. There are several important currency parities in the forex market worldwide. For example, some of the most common currency pairs outside of Eurodollar are:

USD/JPY. This currency pair compares the US dollar with the

Japanese yen.

USD/GBP. This currency pair compares the US dollar with the British pound and is commonly known as the US dollar.

USD/CHF. This currency pair compares the US dollar with the Swiss currency. It's called the Swiss dollar.

USD/CAD. This pair of currencies compare the US dollar with the Canadian dollar.

AUD/USD. This currency pair compares the US dollar with the Australian dollar.

NZD/USD. This currency pair establishes a reconciliation between the New Zealand currency and the US dollar and is called the Kiwi dollar.

There are also currency pairs that are not traded with the US dollar, which are called cross pairs. The common currency pairs share the euro and the Japanese yen.

MINORITY PAIR

Cross-currency pairs or minor currency pairs

Currency pairs that do not include the US dollar are called cross currency pairs or simply "crosses." Traditionally, if we wanted to convert a currency, we would first have to convert the currency into US dollars and then the currency we wanted.

With the introduction of cross-currency, we are no longer forced to make this tired calculation because all brokers now offer direct exchange rates. The most active links come from the three main currencies of the US dollar (the euro, pound sterling, and yen). These currency pairs are also called minors.

Pair of countries

EUR/GBP Euro Zone/United Kingdom

EUR/CHF Euro Zone/Switzerland

EUR/CAD Euro Zone/Canada

EUR/AUD Euro Zone/Australia

EUR/ NZD   Euro Zone/New Zealand

EUR/JPY Euro Zone/Japan

GBP/JPY United Kingdom/Japan

CHF/JPY Switzerland/Japan

CAD/JPY Canada/Japan

AUD/JPY Australia/Japan

NZD/JPY   New Zealand/Japan

GBP/CHF United Kingdom/Switzerland

GBP/AUD United Kingdom/Australia

GBP/CAD United Kingdom/Canada

Exotic currency parity

Exotic currency pairs consist of a larger currency accompanied by the currency of an emerging or strong but smaller economy in a global outlook, such as Hong Kong or Singapore and European countries outside the eurozone.

These pairs are not traded as often as large companies or mines, so the cost of trading them can often be higher than that of large companies or the mine due to lack of liquidity in these markets.

Pair	Countries
EUR/TRY	Euro/Turkish Lira
USD/SEK Dollar	US/Krona Swedish
USD/NOK	US Dollar/Norwegian Krone
USD/DKK Dollar	US/Krone Danish
USD/ZAR Dollar	US/South African Rand
USD/HKD Dollar	US/Hong Kong
USD/SGD Dollar	US/Dollar of Singapore

WHAT IS A FOREX BROKER?

Forex brokers are companies that give businesses access to a platform to buy and sell currencies. Transactions in this market are always done between a pair of different currencies, so forex traders buy or sell the pair they want to trade.

Currency brokers can also be known as sales brokers or currency traders. Most forex brokerage firms only handle a very small portion of the total volume of the forex market. Home traders use these brokers to access the forex market 24 hours a day for speculative purposes. Forex brokerage services are also provided to institutional clients by large companies such as investment banks.

Understand the role of a forex broker

Forex brokers allow access to trade in all major currency pairs; EUR/USD, USD/JPY, GBP/USD, and USD/CHF, as well as the remaining g10 currencies and all exchange rates between them. In addition, most brokers will allow customers to trade currencies in emerging markets.

A forex broker allows the trader to open a deal by buying a currency pair and closing the deal to sell that same pair. For instance, if traders wanted to exchange euros for US dollars, they would include the EUR/USD pair. This is equivalent to buying euros in US dollars for purchase. When they close the trade, they will sell the pair, which will be equivalent to buying the US dollar and using the euro to buy it. If exchange rates were higher when traders closed the transaction, hurting profits, they would otherwise lose money.

Forex brokers have improved customer services over the years. Opening a forex trading account is usually easy and can be done online. Before trading, a forex broker will ask clients to deposit money into their accounts as collateral. However, the broker also provides leverage to clients so that they can negotiate larger amounts than those deposited into their account. Depending on the country where the traders trade, this leverage can be from 30 to 400 times the total available in the trading account. High leverage makes currency trading very risky, and most traders lose money by trying to operate in this way.

How Forex Brokers Make Money

Forex brokers are paid in two ways; first because of the supply and demand of a currency pair differential. For example, when Euro-U.S, the pair of dollars has a bid price of 1,20010 and an asking price of 1,20022, the gap between these two prices is 0.00012, or 1.2 pips. When a retail customer opens a position at the sale price and then closes it at the sale price, the forex broker will charge that amount. Secondly, brokers may charge additional fees. Some may charge for transactions or monthly fees for access to a particular software interface, or fees for access to special commercial products such as exotic options. However, competition between forex brokers is very intense, and most of the companies that serve the trading customers are forced to attract the customers by eliminating the highest possible rates. This has led many to offer free or very low transaction costs that go beyond the margin.

Some forex brokers also make money because of their trading operations. This can be a problem if your operations create a conflict of interest with your customers, but regulation in this area has significantly reduced this practice.

Regulation among forex brokers

Two entities perform regulatory functions between currency exchange agents to deter and abolish fraudulent practices: the Commodity Futures Trading Commission (CFTC) and the National Futures Association (NFA). These organizations publish lawsuits that could go against any practices that are considered fraudulent or intentionally harmful to their clients.

It is worth investigating whether a broker has an excellent reputation and characteristics that are sought after in a broker. This research can be done by visiting the NFA homepage and reviewing Investopedia investor ratings.

Most major Forex brokers allow potential customers to use an exercise account to understand how the system works. It is advisable to try as many options as possible before choosing the broker to use.

THINGS YOU MUST TAKE INTO ACCOUNT BEFORE CHOOSING A FOREX BROKER

There is a lot of money traded daily in the currency markets, making it one of the best investment opportunities.

As a result, the number of brokers increases and, therefore, it is difficult to choose the right broker because of all the advertisements that claim to have the best deal, etc.

Here are some things to consider when choosing a forex broker.

- **Comply with regulations**

Above all, they will be authorized brokers. Speaking to the United States, a recognition forex broker will be a member of the National Futures Association (NFA) and will be officially registered with the Commission on Futures Markets (CFTC) in futures commission trading, such as currency trading.

In addition, NFA is a self-regulated, industry-wide organization in the United States. Its main function is to develop rules, programs, and services to protect the market and its participants. In addition, it is here to ensure that members meet regulatory responsibility and certain obligations.

Do your homework on the broker. Just because a broker looks professional does not mean that his license and regulation are respected.

- **The trading platform**

The trading platform is the investor portal for the market. As such, forex traders have to ensure that the platform can be easily exploited. You may also have all the financial market analysis tools you need to help with your transactions.

More importantly, they will facilitate the entry and exit of businesses. A well-designed trading platform will have a "buy" and "sell" button, and even some will have a "panic" button that locks all open positions. On the other hand, a badly designed interface can generate costly errors when entering commands, such as accidentally adding them in a position instead of closing them, or losing speed when you want to go for a long time.

Other things to consider is including customization options, order entry types, automated trading options, development of elite forex trading strategies, theory testing, and new appreciation trading announcements; so, operators can test the trading platform before opening the financing of an account.

- **Account details**

Although all forex brokers are different, everyone will have offers of similar accounts. Forex participants have access to a variety of broker-based approximation amounts, such as 50:1 or 200:1. Leverage is a loan granted to the account holders by their brokers. For example, taking advantage of 50:1, a currency seller with a US $ 1,000 account can hold a position valued at $ 50,000. The leverage effect favors the operator with winning positions since the profit potential is very great. However, leverage can quickly destroy a merchant's account because it also increases the potential for losses. It leads us to the point that the use of leverage should be used with caution.

A forex broker makes money with established commissions and differentials charging a certain percentage. However, many brokers report that they do not earn commissions and earn their money with wider spreads. For example, the difference could be a fixed difference of three pips, or it may vary depending on market volatility. For example, suppose a GBP/USD price of 1.5551 - 1.5554 has an extension of three pips. This means that once the market participant bought 1.5554, the position has already lost three valuable pips because it could only sell instantly for 1.5551. Therefore, the larger the gap, the more difficult it can be to make a profit. In fact, common pairs like GBP/USD and EUR/USD will generally have narrower divides than weaker pairs.

Most forex accounts can be financed with a very limited initial deposit of up to $50. Of course, with leverage purchasing power, it can be considerably higher than the minimum deposit. This is one of the numerous reasons why currency trading is so attractive to new traders and investors. Many agents offer standard, mini, and micro-accounts with variable initial deposit requirements.

Each forex broker has their own retirement account as well as financing policies. Couriers can authorize account holders to create accounts online through PayPal, simply by credit card or ACH payment method, along with bank transfers, bank checks, or personal or business checks. In general, payments can be made by check or bank transfer. Those are reputable forex brokers and can charge a fee for each service.

- **Execution**

It is imperative that the broker fills the best possible price for your orders. Under normal market conditions (for example, normal liquidity, no press releases or major surprise events), your broker has no reason to say no to the market price you see or very close to the market price. For instance, assuming that you have a stable Internet connection if you click on "buy" EUR/USD for $ 1,300,000, you must be satisfied at this price or under optimal conditions. The speed with which your orders are processed is very important.

A price difference from certain technical problems can make it much more difficult to win this operation.

- **Customer service**

Currency trading is performed 24 hours a day, so a broker's customer service must be available at all times. Therefore, you must choose a broker that you can easily contact in case of problems. Account management or broker technical support skills are as important as their performance in executing transactions.

Agents can be friendly and helpful when opening accounts, but they have excellent after-sales service. When a broker is considered, a quick call can give you an idea of the type of customer service you provide, the waiting times, and the ability of the representative to respond briefly to questions about differentials. leverage, regulation, and details of the company.

BASIC TERMINOLOGIES USED IN FOREX TRADING

What is Lot?

The lot represents the size of your trading operations. In another interpretation, lot is the number of currency units that trade in forex. These include:

- Standard

- Mini batch

- Micro batch

- Nano

What is a full standard?

A standard lot is equal to the 100,000 units of the base currency of a currency trading. A standard lot is similar to the size of the trade. This is one of the three widely known dimensions; The other two are mini batch and micro batch.

In the world of finance, the size of many is a measure of the amount, or increase of a particular asset or product that is considered suitable for purchase and sale. Different types of products are generally available in different batch sizes. Historically, cash exchanges were traded only on specific lots of 100, 1,000, 10,000, or 100,000 units. Lately, though, non-standard lot sizes are also available for forex traders.

A standard lot represents 100,000 units of each currency, while a mini lot represents 10,000 and a micro lot represents 1,000 units of each currency. One movement of a pip for a standard lot is a change of $ 10. For instance, if you buy $ 100,000 against the Japanese yen to ¥ 110.00 and the exchange increases to 110.50 ¥, a movement of 50 pips, you have earned $ 500. otherwise, if the exchange drops 50 pips to ¥ 109.50, your net profit is lost less than $ 500.

With the introduction of online brokers and an increase of competition, small investors can negotiate with amounts that are not a standard, mini, or micro lot. For example, a nano dimension consists of 100 units of a coin. In the interbank market, where banks trade with each other on platforms such as Reuters and EBS, the size of the standard exchange, or a standard lot, is 1 million units in the base currency.

Mini lots: it is often recommended that beginner traders trade with mini, micro, or nano lots to avoid the risk of big losses. A mini lot is equal to 10,000 units, or 10% of a standard lot. Therefore, when a merchant opens an order of 0.1 lot, he negotiates a mini lot.

Why do people use mini lots?

Mini batches may not be interesting in terms of price changes in a company, but they have many practical goals. Therefore, traders also enjoy using mini batches to refine exposure to the market. With the rise of algorithmic trading, the size of the trade is rarely done in blocks, because the risk exposure of 500,000 to 600,000 is quite large, while it can easily go from 500,000 to 510,000.

Traders use mini lots to learn and limit risks

Mini lots are also excellent for traders who learn to trade forex. One misconception shared by many traders is that they can get adequate feedback on their business strategy and their ability to manage risk online using an exercise account. While inputs and outputs and risk management can be refined through a virtual money account, traders generally do not understand how they react to big market movements until real money is at stake.

For the rescue, mini lots help traders know the fluctuations of capital in their account based on market movements. Traders know that the larger the size of transactions, the greater the capital of the account fluctuates absolutely. An example of a gradual adaptation to a situation is the need to use the shallow end of a pool before diving into the bottom to learn how to swim.

Another reason to use mini lots is to limit the risks and test the market. To limit the risks, it is necessary to reduce the size of the exchange on the basis of quantitative models. There is no need for a quantitative model to trade the forex market, but they are common.

Examining the market is something that small sellers like to do because it allows them to "run a business." For example, instead of an operator that immediately opens the size of your planned complete activity, you divide your business into blocks of three. If you were originally going to exchange 30,000 ideas on one idea, they could start with 10,000 and see how it works. If the trade is going well, they could add 10 or leave the 20 in the market. The batch trading method allows you to test your idea with limited risk and is, therefore, a useful tool for transactions of all sizes.

Micro Lot: a micro lot equals 1,000 units, which is 1% of a standard lot. When a trader opens an order of 0.01 lot, he trades a micro lot. For example, buying a lot of 0.01 GBP/USD means buying 1000 GBP. In currency trading, a micro lot equals 1/100 of a specific lot or 1,000 units of the base currency.

To simplify things, if a micro forex is traded in US dollars or euros, each pip will have an approximate value of $ 0.1 in context, compared to $ 10 for a standard lot. Micro-batch trading can be considered as a type of account in which stronger trading is practiced. Let's look at an example: there is a popular online forex broker that provides a micro batch ratio of 400: 1. It is always necessary to review the opposite points of micro batches in currencies to get a clear and concise idea of what they are going to trade?

Advantages of micro lots and forex accounts in the forex market

Before discussing the advantages and disadvantages of micro-batches, it is important to remember that, in the early stages of trading, it was thought that mini-forex accounts would be the best option for beginners. But now, the idea has changed, and forex micro-lot and micro-trading are considered the best way to start trading for beginners.

Advantages:

- Micro accounts can obey the professional rules of money management without taking advantage of the forgotten account.

- Micro lots in micro accounts offer quality commerce with little risk.

- Micro accounts are also useful for testing the effectiveness of currency brokers and for verifying the quality of the platform.

- With micro batches, traders can also use competitive strategies and can also turn to experts to take advantage of diversification without much loss.

Disadvantages of Many Micro Forex

- It is obvious that all have disadvantages. The same goes for micro lots in Forex. The points explained below suggest the disadvantages of micro lots.

- Traders operating with micro lots cannot get technical assistance.

- Traders with joint or commercial accounts will not be able to access them because these accounts are only applicable to the negotiation of property.

Nano Lot: a nano lot, in forex, corresponds to 10 or 100 units. Why is there a difference in unity? Because some forex brokers set the nano at 10 units, while others set it at 100 units. However, nanotechnology is not common. Just a few agents offer it. Normally, nano-batch is the preferred choice of beginners or strategy testing. So, if you buy a new expert advisor or want to try a new strategy, nano-lots will suit you, at least for the first few weeks.

PRICE INTEREST POINT (PIP)

What is a pip? A pip is the movement of the price at a given change. Understanding the change in value helps traders enter or change orders to manage their business strategy.

A pip, abbreviated percentage point, is a very small measure of changing a currency pair in the currency market. It can be measured in terms of quotes or in terms of the underlying currency. A pip is a standardized unit and represents the smallest amount by which a currency quote can change. It is generally equal to USD 0.0001 for currency pairs related to the US dollar, better known as 1/100 of 1%, or base point. This standardized size protects investors against large losses. For example, if the pip were 10 basis points, a change in a pip could lead to greater volatility in currency values.

Calculating the value of a pip when trading in a US dollar account

The world's most traded currency pairs involve the US dollar (USD). When the USD is in second place in a pair, the pip values are fixed and will not change if you have an account activated in US dollars.

The fixed amounts of pip are:

- $ 10 for a standard lot, or 100,000 currency units.

- $ 1 for a mini lot, or 10,000 money units.

- $ 0.10 for a micro lot, representing 1,000 currency units.

These pip values apply to all pairs in which the USD appears in the second part, such as the Euro/US dollar (EUR/USD), British Pound/United States GBP/USD), Australian dollar/US dollar (AUD/USD) and New Zealand Dollar/USD (NZD/USD).

If the USD is not shown in the second place:

Divide the pipe pre-values to the USD/XXX rate.

For instance, to get the pip value of a standard lot for the US dollar/Canadian dollar (USD/CAD) when trading in a US dollar account, divide $ 10 for the USD/CAD exchange. If the USD/CAD rate is 1.2500, the standard pip value of the lot is $ 8, or $ 10 divided by 1.25.

Calculate the pip value for an account that is not USD

Regardless of the currency in which the account is financed, when this coin appears in second place in a pair, pip values are fixed. For instance, if you have a Canadian dollar (CAD) account, any pair that conforms to XXX/CAD, such as USD/CAD, will have a fixed pip value. A standard lot costs $ 10 CAD, a mini lot costs $ 1 CAN, and a micro lot costs $ 0.10 CAN.

To find the value of a pip when the CAD first appears, divide the pip rate set for the exchange. For example, if the exchange rate of the Canadian Dollar/Swiss Franc (CAD/CHF) is 0.7820, a pip is worth $ 1.28 for a mini lot (C $ 1 divided by 0.7820).

If the pair contains the Japanese yen (JPY), for example, the Australian dollar (JPY), you have to multiply the result by 100 after dividing it by the exchange. In fact, for the yen, a pip is 0.01 instead of 0.0001.

For example, if the CAD/JPY price is set to 89.09, to find the standard pip value, divide CAD 10.00 by 89.09, then multiply the result by 100 to obtain a pip value of CAD 11.23.

Follow this process with any currency in the account to find the pip values for parities, including this currency.

Pip value for other currency pairs

In euros

All currency pairs do not include the currency of your account. You may have an account in USD but want to switch to EUR/GBP. Here we show you how to determine the pip value for pairs who do not include the currency of your account.

The second currency is always determined if an individual has an account in that currency. For example, we know that if a person has a GBP account, the EUR/GBP pip value is 10 GBP for a standard lot, as shown above. The next step is to convert 10 GBP to your own currency. If your account is in USD, divide GBP 10 by the USD/GBP fee. If the rate is 0.7600, the pip value is $ 13.16.

If you can only find one quote "back," such as the GBP/USD rate of 1.3152, divide one by the rate to get 0.7600. This is the USD/GBP rate. Then you can do the above calculation.

If the currency of your account is the euro and you want to know the pip value of AUD/CAD, remember that for a person with a CAD account, a standard lot would be 10 CAD for this pair. Convert these $ 10 into euros by dividing by EUR/CAD exchange. If the rate is 1.4813, the standard value of pip from the lot is EUR 6.75.

Always determine which currency provides the pip value: the second currency (AAA). After knowing this, convert the pip value set in this currency by dividing by XXX YYYY, where XXX is the currency of your own account.

BUY AND SELL

Buy a currency pair

When we buy a currency pair, that means that we buy the base currency by selling the valuation currency. Buying EUR/USD means that we buy the euro that sells USD.

Sell a pair of currency

When we sell a currency pair, this means that we sell the base currency, including the valuation currency. Selling EUR/USD means we sell Euros to buy USD.

THE 'BASE' - The base currency

The "basis" for buying or selling is the base currency; in our case, the EUR. The traveler sold before EUR/USD. To do this, he paid (that is, sells) the base currency (Euros) to obtain (that is, buy) equivalent dollars. In the second transaction, he bought the pair EUR/USD. To do this, he redeemed his euros by paying (that is, by selling) the currency of estimation, that is, in dollars.

Summary: purchasing a currency pair simply means buying the base currency by paying or selling the currency, and selling a currency pair implies that we pay (or sell) the base currency to buy the currency. The first currency in the pair is the base currency for immediate reference only.

When to buy and sell forex trading?

The value of currencies is valued or depreciated in relation to other currencies due to differences in supply and demand. In the long run, supply and demand depend on the wellbeing of the economy. If the economy of a country A is better than that of country B, the currency of country A is going to be more in demand and its price will increase. Here the fundamental analysis comes into play. In the short term, prices fluctuate due to short-term speculative trade. Here, technical analysis comes into play.

You can buy the currency pair if you think that the base currency is valued against the quote currency. Similarly, we can sell the pair if we believe the base currency will be DELETED to the valuation currency.

Find yourself in the forex market

In the forex market, you can only use one currency pair when analyzing the price increase of the base currency. As the price increases, you can sell the currency pair to get your winnings.

On the other hand, if your analysis indicates that the price of the base currency should fall, it will sell you the pair first (yes, you don't have it yet) and when the price goes down; then buy again to cover its already sold position to generate its earnings. When he sells it without having it, he simply takes it or lends it to his forex broker and sells it. Then when the price goes down, buy the currency pair to close your trading position.

It is positioned in the forex market when buying or selling a short pair.

• Buy and sell

The basic idea of trading in markets is to buy low and sell high or sell high and buy low. I know this may sounds a little weird to you because you're probably wondering, "how can I sell something I don't have?" However, in the case of an example other than forex, the short sale looks a bit confusing, as if you were selling a stock or a commodity. The basic idea is that your broker will lend you the stock or the merchandise for sale, and then you should buy later to complete the transaction. In the absence of physical shipping, it is possible to sell a title to your broker because it will "come back" later, possibly at a lower price.

• Long vs. short

Another important advantage of the forex market is that it is easier to get earnings from upstream markets when markets go down due to the fact that there is no market bias, such as upward trade bias. Anybody who has traded for a while knows that the quickest money is generated by falling markets. If you learn to trade in the up and down markets, you have a lot of profit opportunities.

LONG: when we take a long position, it means buying the market. Therefore, we want the market to grow so that we can sell our position at a higher price than we buy. This means that I buy the first currency of the pair and sell the second. So, if I buy EURUSD and the euro strengthens against the US dollar, we have a profitable business.

SHORT: when we are short, it means that we sell the market and want the market to come down so that we can buy our position at a lower price than what we sell. This means we sell the first currency of the pair and buy the second. Thus, if we sell GBP/USD and the British pound weakens against the US dollar, we will be profitable.

• Order types

Now is the time to cover the types of orders. When you execute a transaction in the forex market, this is called an "order." There are different types of orders and can vary from one broker to another. Every broker provides certain types of basic orders. However, there are other types of "special" orders not offered by all brokers. We will include all of them below.

Market order: a market order is an order that is placed "on the market" and executed instantly at the best price available.

Limited entry order: a limited entry order is placed to buy below the current market price or sell above the current market price. At first, it is a bit difficult to understand, so let me explain.

If EURUSD is currently trading at 1.3200 and you want to sell the market if it reaches 1.3250, you can place a limited sales order, and then, if the market reaches 1.3250, you will sell. Therefore, the limited sales order is placed above the current market price. If you want to buy the EURUSD at 1.3050 and the market is trading at 1.3100, you will place your purchase order at 1.3050, and if the market reaches this level, it will take a lot. Therefore, the limited purchase order is ALWAYS the current market price.

Stop Entry Order: an entry order is placed to buy above the current market price or to sell below. For example, if you want to operate for a long time but want to enter a resistance zone, you will place your purchase just above the resistance, and you will be provided as the price increases in your stop order. The opposite is true for the input of a seller if he wants to sell the market.

Stop Loss Order: a stop loss order is an order linked to a transaction to avoid additional losses if the price exceeds the specified level. Stop-loss is perhaps the most important order of trading since it allows you to control your risks and limit your losses. This order remains in effect until the item is liquidated or by changing or canceling the stop-loss order.

Stop Trailing: the stop-stop trailing is an order related to the transaction as the standard stop-loss, but a stop-loss move or "trace" the current market price as your transaction evolves. As a general principle, you can set your stop-loss bet at a certain distance from the current market price. Do not start moving until the price is higher than the specified distance. For example, if you set a final stop of 50 pips in EUR/USD, the stop will not advance 51 pips until your position is in favor, then the stop will move again only if the market moves 51 pips so you can be sure that The market moves at your leisure while giving the trade enough room to maneuver to grow and breathe. Scale brakes are best used in markets with a strong trend.

Good to canceled order (GC): a well-canceled order is exactly what it says...valid until canceled. If you submit a BMS order, it will not expire until you cancel it manually. Be careful with them because you do not want to set general conditions, then forget about them so that the market will buy them a month later in a potentially unfavorable position.

Good Day Order (GFD): a "good day order" remains active in the market until the end of the trading day. In forex, trading day ends at 5:00 pm EST or New York time. The exact expiration date of a GFD may vary from one broker to another, so always check with your broker.

Override the Other Command (OCO): one overrides the other command consists of essentially two sets of commands: there may be two entry orders, two arrest orders or two entry orders, and two stop orders. Basically, when one order is executed, the other is canceled. Therefore, if you want to buy or sell EURUSD because you anticipate a pause in consolidation, but you do not know how the market breaks down, you can put a buy-in and a minimum loss on consolidation and a direct sale with stop-loss under consolidation If, for example, the purchase entry is complete, both the sales receipt and the loss of interrupted connection will be immediately canceled. This is a very practical order to use when you do not know in what direction the market will evolve but anticipates a big move.

Draw Another Order (OTO): this command is the opposite of an

OCO command, so instead of canceling one order when it's finished, activate another.

• Lot size/size of contract

In forex, positions are quoted in terms of "a lot." Common nomenclature is "standard lot," "mini lot," "micro lot," and "nano lot."

• How to calculate the pip value

You probably know that currencies are measured in pips, and a pip is the smallest increase in price movement that a currency can move. To make money with these small increases in price movement, you have to trade large amounts of a given currency to see a significant gain (or loss). This is where the lodging comes into play.

So, we must know now how the size of many affects the value of a pip. Let's look at some examples.

Assume that we use standard lots, which control 100,000 units per lot. Let's see how this affects the value of the pip.

1) EUR/JPY at the exchange rate of 100.50 (0.01/100.50) x 100,000 = $ 9.95 per pip

2) USD/CHF at exchange rate of 0.9190 (0.0001/0.9190) x 100,000 = USD 10.88 per pip

In currency pairs where the US dollar is the currency, a standard lot will always be $ 10 per pip, and a mini lot equals $ 1 per pip, a micro-loss equal to 0.10 cents per pip, and a nano-lot will be a penny per pip.

• How to calculate profit and loss

Calculating Financial Data

For now, we calculate profit and loss:

I use a pair without the US dollar as a currency estimate because they are the most delicate:

1) The USD/CHF rate is currently quoted at 0.9191/0.9195. We think we're looking to sell the USD/CHF, which means we will work with the "offer" price of 0.9191 or the rate at which the market is ready to buy.

2) After, selling 1 standard lot (100,000 units) at 0.9191

3) A few days later, the price rises to 0.9091/0.9095 and decides to take its profit in 96 pips, but what is the value of the dollar?

4) The new estimated price for USD/CHF is 0.9091/0.9095. As you close the transaction now, you are using the sales price because you are buying the currency pair to offset the sales order you previously set. Therefore, since the asking price is now 0.9095, this is the price the market is willing to sell for the currency pair or the price at which you can buy it again (since you sold it at the beginning).

5) The difference between the price you were selling at (0.9191)

and the price you want to buy back at (0.9095) is 0.0096, or 96 pips.

6) Using the formula above, we now have (.0001/0.9095) x 100,000 = $ 10.99 per pip x 96 pips = $ 1055.04

For currency pairs where the US dollar is the currency of estimation, calculating the result is fairly straightforward. Just take the amount of pips you have gained or lost and multiply by the dollar you exchange, here is an example:

Suppose you trade EURUSD and buy at 1.3200, but the price drops and stops at 1.3100 ... you just lost 100 pips.

If you trade a standard lot, you would lose $ 1,000 because of a standard pair of US dollars as estimated value = $ 10 per pip and $ 10 per pip x 100 pips = $ 1,000.

If I traded 1 mini lot, I would lose $ 100 because 1 mini USD lot equals $ 1 per pip and $ 1 100 pips = $ 100.

You can also use a forex transaction size calculator.

Always remember that when entering or leaving an operation, you must manage the bid/ask spread. Therefore, when buying a currency, it uses the price of the seller, and when it sells a currency, it uses the price of the buyer.

PRICE OF PRICE AND PRICE

Like any financial market, the currency market has a supply gap. It's just the difference between the price at which you can buy and sell a currency pair. This explains the negative number in the "profit" column as soon as you make a transaction.

Before continuing, let me define the terms "offer price" and "sale price."

OFFER PRICE

Offer Price: used when selling a currency pair. This indicates how much of the quoted currency will be obtained by including a unit of the base currency.

A forex offer price is the price at which the market is ready to buy a specific currency pair in the currency market. This is the price at which the forex trader buys his base currency. In the quote, the Forex Offer Price appears to the left of the currency quote. For example, if the EUR/USD pair is 1.2342/47, the offer price is 1.2342. This means you can sell EUR for $ 1,2342.

SALE PRICE

Check price: used to buy a currency pair. Reflects the amount of the quoted currency to pay to buy a unit of the base currency.

The forex trading price is the price at which the market is willing to sell a certain pair of forex trading currencies in the online forex market. This is the price the merchant buys. It exists to the right of forex trading. For example, in the same EUR/USD pair of 1.2342/47, the reference price is 1.2347. This means you can buy EUR for $ 1,2347.

Propagation

A spread is a conventional concept for financial markets. It represents only the price difference between the price at which an operator can buy or sell an underlying asset.

You have certainly experienced the spread when you arrive at a bank or exchange office to get the foreign exchange. The bank always shows two exchange rates: one that accepts purchase and one that is ready to sell. The difference between these two prices is the bank's income from the currency transactions it performs for you.

Bid-Ask = propagation

There are two types of currency prices in forex: bid and ask.

The price we pay to buy the pair is ask. It is always a little higher than the market price. The price at which we sell the pair in Forex is called bid. It is always a little lower than the market price.

The price we see in the graph is always a bid price. The selling price is always higher than the price offered by some pips. The difference is the difference between these two prices. In other words, it's a commission that you pay your agent for each transaction.

SPREAD = ASC - IDB

For example, the EUR/USD bid/ask exchange rate is 1.1250/1.1251. Buy the pair at the lowest price of 1.1251 and sell at the lowest price of 1.1250. This represents a difference of 1 pip.

When you click on the "New Order" button, a window will

appear where you can define the details of your transaction. The window will also show the current prices of supply and demand.

Types of propagation

The types of propagation depend on the broker's policy. A spread can be fixed or floating.

Fixed differential

Fixed spreads remain the same no matter of market conditions at any given time. That way, you know in advance how much you will pay for an exchange. Another good thing is that the broker will not be able to widen the gap even if the market conditions change.

Floats

Floating or floating spreads, on the other hand, are constantly changing. They will be expanded or reduced depending on the supply and demand of currencies and the general volatility of the market. Float spreads generally increase during periods of higher economic recovery, and during the holidays when the amount of liquidity in the market decreases. Variable differentials eliminate experience requirements and, when the market is calm, can be lower than fixed ones.

How to choose the optimal spread

The optimal type of dissemination depends on your preferences as a business. In general, traders with smaller accounts that operate less frequently will benefit from fixed margin prices. Operators with larger accounts that often operate during peak market hours (when spreads are tighter) and want a quick balance of operations will benefit from variable spreads.

Calculation of cost

Keep in mind that the cost of spreading in forex is generally insignificant compared to expenses in stock markets or options. Since the differential is expressed in pips, an operator can easily calculate the cost of each transaction to multiply the spread of the pip by the value of a pip. How to calculate the benefit?

Propagation is a significant parameter to consider when choosing a broker. Make sure you are comfortable with the spreads offered. Bear in mind that you can also try the business terms of the company without investing your money by opening a demo account.

The shorter the periods of your profession, the larger is the size of an extension. For example, if you hold an open position for several minutes and your profit is 10 pips, a 3 pips spread would mean that you will pay 30% of your profits for the execution of this transaction. If you keep your operation open for a day, the price will probably change even more; suppose you earn 100 pips. In this case, you will only pay 3% of your earnings as a differential.

The more popular the currency pair, the smaller the gap. For example, the spread of EUR/USD operations is generally very low or, as operators say, tight.

ADVANTAGES OF FOREX OVER OTHER INVESTMENT ASSETS

Currency trading, like most trading activities, can have favorable and unfavorable characteristics for traders. People looking to get into the forex market will have to weigh the pros and cons of currencies to decide if it is an attractive market and suited to their needs.

ADVANTAGES

Even though forex trading carries some risks, it still has many benefits that can turn it into a profitable and attractive company. These include the following:

• Accessibility

The forex market is one of the most accessible markets for individual traders. Traders can set up a forex account in one or three days and start trading at £ 50. Most brokers can trade online, and traders have access to real-time market prices, news, price charts, tools, and strategies through online trading platforms. Additionaly, the forex market is open 24 hours a day/5 days a week, which means that trading transactions can be more easily included in the trading calendar than other types of trading.

• Leads

Access to leverage can mean the difference between small business profits and big profits. The availability of resources to take advantage of the exchange market is greater than in most other markets. Depending on their country of origin, traders can access a leveraged margin of 100: 1 or more on the initial capital invested in an operation.

• Potential for fast returns

The currency market is changing rapidly and has extreme liquidity. These characteristics, combined with the generally greater leverage available to traders, mean that there may be faster returns in the forex market than in other markets, where traders are looking for organic "growth" in the value of their trading.

• Easy to sell

Short selling in some markets may require the borrowing of assets and risk exposure of the owner in demand for a short position, but short selling of currencies is simpler. Currencies are bought and sold in pairs, which means that when one trader buys one, he sells another. Traders who speculate that a currency will lose value only need to sell that currency and buy another, with no loans in the process.

• Liquidity

The forex market is the largest market in the world. This means that there is generally a lot of money to trade, especially in major currencies. Traders working with the trading table model in currency exchange offices are usually offered enough liquidity since the normal broker takes the opposite position of a transaction when liquidity can be low in other parts of the market

• Technical strategy

The forex market lends itself nicely to technical analysis. While stock and bond traders may need to deepen the fundamentals and financial health of stock issuers and securities to ensure that their securities are profitable, forex traders can take advantage by using technical analysis of stock prices.

In contrast to the fundamental analysis, which requires detailed background information about the financial health of the assets, the technical analysis is based on historical prices and trends that provide clues about the perception of supply and demand of the market, and also of the opinion of these goods.

• Lower level of internal price manipulation.

Equity markets, securities, and even assets are often heavily influenced by private information held by insiders and key players in those assets. However, control of the currency market is much less centralized and less influenced by inside information.

In most cases, the holders of any possible "internal information" about possible exchange movements are government officials or central bank authorities who are usually subject to a public record and are generally subject to strict government surveillance. This aspect of forex makes them one of the most transparent markets for trading.

• Fewer fees and commissions

Trading in stocks, bonds, mutual funds, and other instruments is often subject to heavy commissions and sometimes hidden fees that can make transactions more expensive than expected.

In many cases, the costs of buying and selling currencies are determined solely by the differential of supply and demand, which is the difference between the prices of the offer (buyer) and the seller (seller) clearly published by real-time broker. This is another aspect of trading operation that makes it more transparent.

• Simple tax rules

While traders in other markets may be required to keep special tabs on their short-term and long-term business activities for tax purposes, currency trading is often subject to simpler tax rules that facilitate calculations.

• Automation

Forex trading also adapts well to automated trading strategies. With some studies, forex traders can configure automated transactions, programming entries, stop-loss, and price limits before making a transaction; or ask the platform to negotiate certain price movements or other market conditions.

An operator with a well-designed automated strategy can take advantage of daily market fluctuations without exhausting their physical and mental faculties to establish transactions to keep up with the latest market developments.

PSYCHOLOGY OF A FOREX TRADER

Forex Trading Psychology

The psychology of exchange operations is a big thing. Often, it is psychology, and not the lack of academic knowledge or application skills, that is considered the main creator of business errors. Financial operators are constantly repeating the mistakes made by operators of various national, cultural, and social backgrounds, suggesting that they are the common characteristics shared between us as humans that are at the root of these mistakes.

This common function is fear, which creates the "fight or flight" response in humans. Unfortunately, it is this fight or flight reaction that can cause many traders to crash. We can't change how we feel for millions of years, but we can change the way we approach these feelings by examining the psychology of successful forex traders and then utilizing the results. We will examine how we behave and react to business situations from the point of view of the psychology of currency trading.

Fear can have a significant limiting effect on business behavior. Of course, your mind will want to find the safest option to ensure its survival. In terms of trading, this implies that if an operation seems to lose profits, its natural instinct would be to withdraw from the operation so that it does not cause additional losses.

However, this can move away from a carefully planned business strategy. Worse, it could lead to reckless decisions, hoping to turn that lost operation into a lot more money than if you just let it play. Instead of focusing on the long-term plan, your mind needs to focus on making the most of this short-term losing stance.

Recognizing the role of psychology in forex trading can help alleviate the fear of your decision-making process. Knowing the fear in the act allows you to act, both business and individual. This will also allow you to restore control of logic and reason, which is your ultimate goal.

• Greed

The greed demon is the number one enemy of forex traders. This demon has a very long, pointed tongue that constantly whispers that opportunity in the market disappears unless we act quickly to capture it. His feet are on fire: he screams "faster, faster" at the shop, urging him, causing him to lose concentration. He has an empty stomach; he is emaciated, weak, and hungry because none of his exhortations to accelerate and greed ultimately lead to the slightest benefit.

It may be natural that most forex traders are money and profit-oriented individuals who value financial success. It is true that without a strong desire to make money, no trader can resist the pressure of trade in the currency market. For moderate amounts, the pursuit of monetary gain and the pursuit of financial success are solid and necessary. But these healthy impulses become unhealthy when driving our business decisions: the devil of greed must know his place and should not interfere in business practices that must be formulated only by logic.

How to avoid the bad choices that greed imposes on us? The first step to overcome greed is to adopt a disciplined approach to negotiation that minimizes the role of the moment in our negotiation decisions. By formulating a business strategy at the outset and remaining loyal throughout an exchange, we can ensure that greed has no choice but to bow quietly as we study the markets and make decisions based on reason and analysis.

Success can be achieved through a sophisticated business method and disciplined application. Emotions grow where uncertainty and fear are common. To avoid such a situation, we ensure that our responses to market developments are assessed and based on the principles established by our diligent study. Since our mere motivation or willingness to make a profit will not ensure that we take them, there is nothing to be gained from hearing the teachings of the devil of greed.

Euphoria

The queen of forex demons, Euphoria, is a creature that promises infinite wealth and generates boundless misery. Euphoria strives to ensure that where we look, we see only wonderful prospects of unlimited profits. This is how the merchant received the Midas Touch, the success being the natural consequence of his usual behavior.

Under normal circumstances, euphoria is not important to most traders because everyone is aware that the success of currency trading is not a child's play. Although great benefits can be obtained in a short time, they are usually the result of a period of study and practice in which it was proven time and time again that false promise of euphoria lacked in direction. In the case of the beginner, who does not have this background of hard work and study, the euphoria may be the result of a series of profitable exchanges, because the business ends up believing that their knowledge of the markets is impeccable.

The key here is to know that the first requirement for the perfect analysis is to assume that no analysis is perfect. Therefore, the successful analyst or marketer is always skeptical about the value of their explanations, even if they do not hesitate to apply them because they base their work solely on logic. The potential for earning the next trade is independent of previous profitability. So, it does not make sense to be enthusiastic about earning: the next transaction may or may not be profitable, depending on the diligence with which our market research has been undertaken.

Therefore, the best way to avoid euphoria is to understand that a series of gains or losses do not affect the outcome of the next trade we will make. The success or failure of the next operation depends solely on our ability to exclude the excitement of our market research. It is in this knowledge that the alpha and omega of a successful business strategy are found.

Panic

Panic is the opposite of euphoria. In a panic situation, the trader only sees losses in the market, without the possibility of concluding a profitable business. This is an exceptionally weird way of thinking about the currency market since, by definition, someone's loss must be the gain of another person. When a trader loses large sums in a large currency transaction, another trader can earn significant profits in a short trade in the same pair. This in itself should help traders be more realistic about panic attacks in the forex market, but experience indicates that this is not the case.

So what are the causes of panic that drives a currency trader to make bad decisions? Clearly, periods of market volatility are the most common drivers of a panic reaction. As price fluctuations rise in depth and frequency, the value of forecasts decreases considerably. This leads to a loss of confidence in our business choices and, if the period lasts long enough, the inevitable emotional outcome will panic in most cases.

A panicked business will make all kinds of mistakes. It will close a profitable position in the hope that it will invest quickly and record losses soon. He could not do a logical analysis of his situation and became a victim of mental illusions regarding "potential" scenarios. The market is the ultimate arbiter of the success or failure of a transaction, but for the trader to panic, all kinds of imaginary references, unrealistic expectations are the main criterion for the relevance and final profitability of a transaction. The effect of panic is greatly increased by leverage, and the damage caused by it intensifies with tight scales.

To address issues related to business psychology, we will minimize the role of emotions in our business decisions. To diminish the role of emotions, we must understand that success or failure are not related to luck, but the logical consequences of our choices. Earlier, we discussed that it is almost impossible to delete an unaccounted account after a single transaction. If the merchant manages to create an empty account after a series of lost transactions, it is difficult to speak of fate or luck as the cause of the disaster. Leverage is completely under the control of the account holder; You can define at any value, as long as you can give the consequences. Leverage amplifies the profit/loss potential of a trade, but it also exaggerates the emotional aspect of the trade. Ultimately, this intensification of emotional pressure may be the most dangerous and negative impact of leverage.

The best way to deal with emotional problems is to get a logical approach to trading. The best way to acquire this attitude is to understand the market mechanisms and forces driving economic activity. In this book, we try to provide you with a basic understanding of the factors on which you can build your knowledge to improve your potential for success in the forex market.

WHAT IS A FOREX TRADING STRATEGY?

A forex trading strategy defines a system used by a forex trader to determine when to buy or sell a currency pair. Traders can use various currency strategies, including technical analysis or fundamental analysis. A good business strategy allows the trader to analyze the market and execute transactions with confidence using proven risk management techniques.

Basics of a Forex Trading Strategy

Currency trading strategies can be manual or automated methods for generating trading signals. Manual systems involve a merchant sitting in front of a computer screen, searching for trading signals and interpreting whether to buy or sell. Automated systems involve a businessman who develops an algorithm that finds business signals and executes the transactions themselves. These systems eliminate human emotions from the equation and can improve performance.

Traders must be cautious when purchasing standard currency trading strategies, as it is difficult to verify their history, and many successful trading systems are kept secret.

Create a currency trading strategy

Many operators start with a simple business strategy. For example, you may notice that a specific currency pair tends to recover from a particular level of support or resistance. Then they can decide to add other elements that will improve the accuracy of these business signals over time. For example, they may ask that the price be recovered by a certain percentage or by a number of pips of a specific support level.

An effective forex trading strategy has several different components:

Market Selection – Traders will determine which currency pairs to trade and become experts at reading these currency pairs.

Position size – Traders must determine the size of each position to control the amount of risk assumed in each individual transaction.

Entry Points – Traders should develop rules that regulate when to enter a long or short position in a given currency pair.

Exit points – Operators must develop rules that tell them when to exit a long or short position and when to exit a loss position.

Business tactics – Operators will have definite rules for buying and selling currency packages, including the selection of suitable execution technologies.

Marketers will consider developing business systems in programs such as MetaTrader that facilitate the automation of rule tracking. In addition, these applications allow operators to analyze their business strategies to determine their past performance.

When Is It Time to Change Strategies?

A forex trading strategy works especially well when traders follow the rules. But, like anything else, a particular strategy may not always be unique, and so what works today may not necessarily work tomorrow. If a strategy is not profitable and does not produce the desired results, operators can consider the following before modifying a game plan.

Adapt risk management to the trading style: if the risk/reward ratio is not appropriate, this can lead to a change in strategy.

Market conditions change: a business strategy may depend on specific market trends. Therefore, if they change, a particular strategy may become obsolete. This could indicate the need for adjustments or modifications.

Understand: if an operator doesn't understand the strategy, there's a good chance it won't work. If a problem arises or if an operator does not know the rules, the effectiveness of the strategy is lost.

Although change can be good, changing a forex trading strategy can often be expensive. If you change your strategy too often, you run the risk of losing.

FOREX TRADING STYLES AND STRATEGIES

There are several types of trading styles (described below), ranging from short to long term. They have been widely used in previous years and remain a popular choice among the list of the best forex trading strategies in 2020. The best forex traders always know different styles and strategies in their search for forex trading, so you can pick the right one according to the market conditions.

Scalping: these are very short operations, which can only be maintained for a few minutes. A seller tries to quickly resolve the gap between offers and offers and only runs a few profit points before closing. This strategy generally uses check cards, such as those found in MetaTrader 4 Supreme Edition. This trading platform also offers some of the best forex indicators for scalping. In addition, the forex 1-minute trading strategy can be seen as an example of this style of trading.

Trading Day: these are transactions that end before the end of the day, as the name implies. This eliminates the risk of being negatively affected by significant movements during the night. Today's trading strategies are usually the perfect forex trading strategies for beginners. Transactions can only take a few hours, and price bargains on charts can usually be defined in one to two minutes. The exchange of 50 pips a day is a good example of a daily trading strategy.

Swing Trading: positions held for several days, in which traders seek to take advantage of the short-term price structure. A swing business can usually look at the bars every half hour or hour.

Trading positions: following the long-term trend, trying to maximize profits resulting from significant price changes. A long-term operator will generally search the charts at the end of the day. The best position negotiation strategies require immense patience and discipline from the operators. This requires a good understanding of the fundamentals of the market.

Trading strategies in new currencies.

Then there are the new forex trading systems. Whether you want to trade non-monthly wages or wage decisions on wages or interest rates, these strategies and currency trading systems are what you need to do.

Commercial food can be profitable and extremely risky.

If you do not know how to do it, do not exchange news. You can delete your business account in seconds to minutes because the course can fluctuate so fast that it will take you off guard.

But if you do not use forex information exchange strategies that are in use today, it is best to check daily before negotiating which major press releases are supposed to be published and then decide if you are waiting for news to be published, so just do the transactions for another day.

Here are some forex trading strategies where you can use to exchange forex news:

- One-minute forex news trading strategy

- Best interest rate trading strategy

- Negotiation strategy for non-agricultural wage news

- Forex countertrend strategies

Contract strategies are based on the fact that most reviews do not become long-term trends. Therefore, an operator using this strategy seeks to take advantage of the price trend to recover from the ups and downs set out above. On paper, counter-trend strategies are the best forex trading strategies to increase confidence because they have high success.

However, it is important to remember that risk management requires strict rules. These forex trading strategies are based on the levels of support and resistance. But there is also the risk of significant inconvenience when these levels decrease. Constant market monitoring is a good idea. The market condition that best fits this type of strategy is stable and volatile. This type of market environment offers fluctuations in healthy prices that are limited in a range. It is important to remember that the market may change.

For example, a stable and calm market could start to follow a trend while they are stable and then become volatile as the trend develops. The evolution of a market can be uncertain. You need to look for current state evidence to find out if this fits your business style.

Upcoming trends strategies

Sometimes, a market leaves a fork, going under support or over the resistance to start a trend. How can this happen? As support breaks down and the market reaches new lows, buyers begin to wait. In fact, buyers are constantly discovering that lower prices are being charged and want to wait until they reach the floor. At the same time, there will be traders who will approach or simply be forced to leave their positions.

The trend continues until sales run out, and buyers' belief is restored to reality when it is determined that prices will no longer drop. Strategies that follow the trends encourage traders to buy in markets once they have surpassed resistance and sold markets and have fallen to support levels.

In addition, trends can be dramatic and protracted. Due to the breadth of the movements involved, this type of system has the potential to be the forex trading strategy of success. Trend systems use indicators to inform traders about opening a new trend, but of course, there is no sure way to know.

Here's the good news:

If the indicator can set a time when there is a greater probability that a trend will start, the odds will change in favor. The indication that a trend is forming is called a pause. A getaway occurs when the price is higher or lower for a specific number of days. For example, an upward 20-day flight occurs when the price exceeds the highest of the last 20 days.

Trend systems require a particular mindset, due to the long run, during which profits may disappear as the market fluctuates, these transactions may be more psychologically demanding. As markets are volatile, trends will tend to be more skewed, and price fluctuations will be greater. Therefore, a trend tracking system is the best trading strategy for forex markets that are silent and evolving.

A Donchiana trend system is a good example of a simple trend tracking strategy. Donchian chains have been invented by future distributor Richard Donchian and are indicators of established trends. The Donchian channel settings can be changed as you wish, but for this example, we will talk about a discussion in 20 days.

After all, an escape from the Donchiana chain suggests one of two things:

Buy if the price of a market exceeds the previous 20 days;

Sell if the price is lower than the minimum of the previous 20 days.

There is an additional rule for trading when the market condition is most favorable to the system. This rule is intended to filter out eruptions that go against the long-term trend. In summary, look at the 25-day moving average and the 300-day moving average. The address of the shortest moving average determines the allowed address. This rule says you can only go:

Short if the 25-day moving average is below the 300-day moving average

Long if the 25-day moving average is above the 300-day

moving average

Transactions end in the same way but using only 10-day workshops. This means that if you open a long position and the market is below the last 10 days, you may want to sell to leave the transaction, and vice versa.

PRICE ACTION TRADING

Stock market trading involves the study of historical prices for the formulation of technical trading strategies. The price action can be used alone or together with an indicator. Fundamental principles are rarely used. However, it is not uncommon to incorporate economic events as a justification factor. As noted above, many other strategies fall within the price range.

Transaction time:

Stock price trading can be used in different periods (long, medium, and short). The ability to use multiple shipping times for analysis makes trading the price action appreciated by many traders.

Entry Points/Exit:

There are several methods to determine the support/resistance levels that are generally used as input/output points:

- Fibonacci

- Use bad candles

- Trend identification

- Indicators

- Oscillators

Within price action, there is trading for the holder, the trend, the day, scalping, swing, and position. These strategies respond to the various forms of business requirements that will be detailed below. The examples illustrate several techniques for trading these strategies to demonstrate how trading can be diversified and a variety of customized options that traders can choose from.

Daily Forex Card Strategy

The best forex traders bet on everyday graphs and short-term strategies. Compared to the one-hour currency trading strategy, or even those with shorter trading times, everyday cards are less buzz. Such charts can give you over 100 pips a day because of their longer workout, which could lead to some of the best forex tradings.

The business signs are more reliable, and the potential for profit is much greater. Merchants also don't have to worry about daily news and random price fluctuations. The method is based on three main principles:

1. Trend situation: markets tend to consolidate, and this process is repeated in cycles. The first principle of this style is to find long-term movements in the currency markets. One of the ways to identify forex trends is to study 180 forex data periods. Identifying the ups and

downs of the swing will be the next step. Referring to this price data in the current charts, you can identify the direction of the market.

2. Be warned: be patient, and you will rule out the need to enter the market immediately. You need to stay out and preserve your capital for a greater opportunity.

3. Less leverage and greater stop-loss: keep in mind the strong market fluctuations during the day. However, using larger positions does not mean danger to large amounts of capital.

Although many trade strategy guides are available for professional forex traders, the best currency trading strategy for consistent trading can be achieved only through extensive practices. Here are some other strategies you can try:

Hourly business strategy

You can take advantage of the 60-minute delay in this strategy. The easiest currency pairs to trade with this strategy are EUR/USD, USD/ JPY, GBP/USD, and AUD/USD. It would need a 100pips pulse indicator and arrow indicator; both are available in MetaTrader 4.

Purchase Rules:

You can enter a long position when these two conditions are met:

The Momentum 100 pips indicator activates a buy signal when

its blue line crosses the red line below.

The arrow indicator gives a green arrow sign.

In this case, you can place the stop loss below the red indicator line or the most recent support line. You can close the transaction after 30 pips, or get profits when the arrows indicate a red arrow.

Sales Rules:

You can enter a short position when the following conditions are met:

- The Momentum 100 pips indicator activates a sales signal when its blue line crosses the red line from above.

- The arrow keys give a red arrow sign.

Place stop loss above the red indicator line or last resistance line. Close the operation after 30 pips or when the arrows indicate a green arrow sign.

Weekly Forex Trading Strategy

While many forex traders favor intraday trading because market volatility offers more profit opportunities in shorter terms, the weekly currency trading strategy can offer greater flexibility and stability. A weekly candle provides detailed market information. It contains five candles and daily changes that reflect current market trends. Weekly forex trading strategies are built on lower position dimensions and avoiding excessive risks.

For this strategy, we will use the Mobile Exponential Indicator

(EMA). Last week's last candle should be closed at a level higher than the EMA value. Now you have to look for the moment where the maximum level of the past week was exceeded. Then, a stop purchase order is placed on the closed H4 candle, at the price level of the broken level.

The stop loss must be set to the nearest minimum point, between 50 and 105 pips. The preceding extreme value is used for calculations if the nearest minimum point is less than 50 pips. Here, the framework of the move last week is taken as a range of profits.

MAKING AN EFFECTIVE TRADING PLAN

The time has come to decide what and when to trade. It's time to develop your business plan. Please, don't put your faith and hard-earned money into a black box system that is more likely to be just a moving average system. It is important that you know why you make the transactions you make.

If you are not willing to work on creating your own business plan, I think it would be best for you to deposit your money in a managed account, only to have the opportunity to fight in that difficult arena.

The first step in developing your own business plan is to work hard and develop your own business style, not mine, not a combination, presentation, or even a smart website marketer. When defining your trading style, it should be up to you and you alone.

Developing a business plan is very similar to a business plan. It is a device that allows you to define how you think about managing your business. A business plan describes how to do the transactions. Time, price, volume, and news are essential elements of trading. Even if your business plan is not necessarily for others, it is your responsibility to inform and confirm how you hope to achieve it.

Include goals in your plan: three months, six months, one year, two years, five years, 10 years,

Elements to consider

- What time of day is trading (which sessions)?

- What currency pair do you want to track?

- Do you operate in the event of market fluctuations (fundamental news announcements)?

- How long do you go to practice your business?

- How much are you ready to risk in the markets?

The basics of a business plan

There are several essentials that you can consider in your business plan. These essentials lay the groundwork for your plan and help you achieve your goals. Here are some key things you can include:

- Indicate your purpose

- Why do you want to trade in the forex market?

- What do you expect to gain from the business?

- What are your business goals?

- How do you think about becoming a better traitor?

- How do you use your business plan?

- Clearly define your business and investment goals.

- Indicate your goals and what you expect to achieve and achieve through trade.

Purchase strategy

• How do you find which pairs to exchange?

Examples:

News, research, technical analysis, fundamental analysis, etc.

• How to finish your "shopping list" (currency pairs on your own)

Are you thinking of buying a radar)?

• Use of technical analysis: you need to understand what you are looking at. Understand the indicators you use and what they measure. Your preferred indicator may not be useful in many situations. In fact, I recommend using a series of indicators instead of just one. You should know when to use techniques and when not to use them.

• Use of fundamental analysis: fundamental information announcements can initiate the most volatile movements in this market. Make sure you understand how the basics work.

Sales strategy

• Set a desired minimum target for each operation. You can make 20 pips per transaction or 50 pips per transaction. Define a goal that suits you and follow.

• Use stop-loss orders to reduce the risk of automatically selling to a lower defect price. Interestingly, this is a very controversial problem. Earlier, I did not even trade parades. Recently, the euro and the pound have taught me difficult lessons, and I'm incorporating steps into my strategy in the future.

• How much are they willing to lose if this trade goes bad?

• Some traders continually increase stop-loss prices as they trade

Go in your direction

This is called a shock bet and can be a very useful tool for securing profits and reducing risk.

Strategy to wait

• What will you do if the price does not move after the purchase? Sell and move on, or hold or wait for action?

• Some operators will remain in business until the activity and volume recover. They feel they are waiting for comfort. This action may require more capital in your business account, which may require you to maintain multiple non-mobile transactions.

Money and risk management.

• How will you limit your risks?

• How will you make the total value of your account maximum?

• Research money management techniques: there are many.

This may include how much money or percentage of the total value of your portfolio to use in each transaction.

• Margin: margin can be a very useful tool for many operators, but it can be frightening and risky if not used properly. You can receive a margin call from your broker anytime, which means you want to collect your money now. The margin gives you additional purchasing power. The margin also gives you an additional risk. Use the margin wisely and wisely. Some traders never take the edge.

As the Scouts say, get ready.

Forex Trader Preparation

It means developing your plan, developing your strategies, testing your techniques, and continually improving everything. The process never really ends, and there are good business opportunities to take advantage of. Having a well thought out plan is a solid basis for a beginner operator. Commit to your plan and fulfill it. As I said before, exchange tips on a demo account until you see decent returns. Later, start trading micro lots in a mini account. This will ensure that your plan is based on principles and will benefit you in the long term.

How much do you have to exchange?

There are many negotiation strategies that most of them work in some situations and not in others. There are forums, newsgroups and an internal software industry that has developed around the idea that the most important point is the entry point.

The fact is that the starting point and money management are more important than the entrance. is

Starting a transaction is one thing, and another is when you know and determine how much you are willing to risk. Think of it this way, place transactions at random points on the chart (by the way, which I don't recommend). Suppose this is a coincidence and that 50% of the transactions are potentially profitable, and 50% of the transactions are nonprofit.

If you used a 10 pips stop benefit and a 20 pips benefit, you could actually earn money because half of your transactions would be more positive for your failures than for losses. Now, you understand that this is an extremely simplistic and naive way of thinking about it and instead illustrates a point. All exchanges do not earn 20 pips without returning to their stop loss. His money management techniques would be a little stronger than my example.

Your investment in forex should represent only about 10% of your venture capital. Remember that this is the riskiest way to invest in your portfolio. Therefore, do not pay your full retirement fund in forex. Also, do not consider forex as a way to make a living if you were just fired.

So, if you have $ 100,000 in venture capital (venture capital is money you can afford to lose, not your pension fund and certainly not your home), then you should feel free to invest $ 10,000 in the market. However, if you are like many Americans and have only $ 10,000 or less in venture capital, do not invest more than $ 1,000 in this market. The total amount you need to use to enter the market must be approximately 5% of the total capital of your account. If you operate with a $ 10,000 account, do not use more than $ 500 of your shares in the market (about five mini lots).

If your account is $ 1,000, you should exercise caution when operating more than half of a minimum. At the same time, this may seem too conservative. Honestly, I have a $ 500 mini account and four or five mini accounts open at the same time; But this is not fully detected. Like many operators, I felt the edge of the margin call. Slow and stable should be growing.

What are the most active moments for the exchange?

It's fun, I talk to traders all over the world, and everyone feels that the best time to trade is two in the morning. If you think about it, two o'clock in the morning may not be the best time in the world, can it? So what's the best time swap? The best moments to trade in the forex market are when there is more than one open market, which results in more volume and liquidity.

It is obvious that someone sells currencies anywhere in the world at any time of the week. When one market closes, another opens. The market starts its week in New Zealand, followed by Australia, Asia, the Middle East, Europe, and then America. US markets and the UK accounts for about half of all trading in the market, and about two-thirds of New York's trading activity is done in the morning, while European markets are still open.

Forex market volume remains high throughout the day, but trading is usually more intense when the major markets overlap. As a result, the likelihood of strong market change is higher during these periods.

What pair do you have to exchange?

Most currency trading currencies involve the US dollar against another currency. The US economy has always been considered the largest in the world. The Japanese yen and the Swiss franc were also the basis of many transactions. Each of these markets has very distinctive characteristics.

Dollars

The US dollar has experienced violent fluctuations, and the credibility of US economic policy has been questioned many times. After the Plaza Accord, the US dollar has fallen aggressively.

Japanese Yen

The yen has been volatile in recent years and strengthened in the 1990s; However, in recent years or so, the problem of appreciation of the contraction of export trade has encouraged volatility.

Swiss Francon

The independent and neutral political position of the Swiss

banking system allows the Swiss to serve as a refuge. This combination resulted in tickets to Swiss francs in times of insecurity and turmoil.

How do you choose a profit that takes a profit or a stop loss?

Probably, you have identified a period of time that you are interested in trading and one or two currency pairs that you have promised to study. Now is the time to identify what you want to do and what you are willing to lose for transactions. Don't attack any illusions here; you will lose and lose regularly. The key is to lose good. There are a number of theories about profit-making and loss-making. I think knowing when leaving a business is almost as important as knowing when to enter a business, but it pays less attention. I think it comes from the fact that it's a bit subjective. It really depends on your period, your currency pair, and what happens to your peer during the chosen period.

We recommend building your own table every few months. The market changes over time; Therefore, do not get caught up with old data in your analysis. A caveat before digging in here. Just because a pair has a wide range of business in one session doesn't mean it's the best pair for business. GBP/JPY has a large trading margin. It is an extremely volatile pair that has taken more than a few dollars.

What I'm saying here is that there are different legs for different parties at different periods. For example, establishing a profit of 30 pips in an AUD/USD exchange placed in the overlap between Europe and Asia would be a bit ridiculous, since the pair only has an average range of 20 pips in this period.

Let's say your chosen trading system is correct in 50% of the cases. If your winning catches are usually 30 pips and your stop-loss is 15 pips, then you would be a profitable trader.

Another method to identify stop loss is to use common indicators as exit strategies. One such indicator is the satellite dish.

How far is it?

As you can imagine, you need a lot of time and resources to look back at your charts. It is also generally said that the market has a limited memory, which means that looking too much at the charts is not really relevant. This has serious consequences for volatile currency volatility and, in particular, for unstable market conditions. The basic principle is that you should only keep the last x number of candles on your table. The number x is determined by its period, currency pair, and volatility.

I have attended several seminars presented by different experts, and each has slightly different ideas on how it should work. I like to see the last 100 candles of a given card. This does not mean that you do not look at the different periods when trading. I find it useful to look at daily charts and to look at shorter and shorter times. Even though I keep the 15- and 30-minute charts, I personally like to swap the one-hour charts.

As in the whole business, these models should be used with the indicator, its trend lines, its support and resistance lines, or one of its combinations. It's easy to get a single sign up and jump into an operation without getting confirmation from another source, which includes basic news announcements. Hundreds of candle models have been identified and documented. I think learning how to identify these particular patterns is a great step in integrating candles into your business style.

What time should I watch?

Well, that's all. It depends on your time commitments. It depends on your temper. Can you go to sleep in an open tent? Will you be able to manage the market going forward while you need to rest? Otherwise, it would be better to do short-term operations and see 5-minute, 30-minute, or 1-hour charts. Have patience, you can wait.

If not, again, you may be happier trading in the short-term charts. It also depends on the size of your initial account. A larger account can handle potential fluctuations that can occur in long-term transactions.

What will my daily goal be in terms of profit or loss?

This is an intriguing question. The first response you are likely to give is that you only want profits and not losses. Unfortunately, this is not always possible. and if you commit zero losses, you automatically fail and end up hurting your head when you suffer a loss. You will also wish to make your daily profit goals realistic: you do not need to create stress with impossible goals.

When choosing your daily profit and loss goals, you must consider the power of compound capital. For example, the first month, you have to earn $ 100 .1 in trade. This one is equivalent to about 50 pipes a day. If there were 20 trading days that month, it is possible to reach 50 pips a day. But we also consider it a little high, depending on your partner and your program.

The other key I want to address with this goal is that most platforms and brokers will only allow you to exchange a maximum of fights at a time, say 50. So, a place in your third year will open up a lot. positions at the time to try to reach this gain of 50 pips.

I also believe that by following this "system," you will not lose and optimize your account. So, be sensible about your goals and I think you will be pleasantly surprised. I don't think it's surprising that the most successful (long-term) negotiations are that they have been in the market for years.

Being out of the market can be a good plan

When establishing your business plan, you need to take a short break. If you set the pace too fast, you run the risk of running out or rewriting your plan shortly after the start of your transactions. Being out of the market may be good for many reasons. One of the reasons is that you always have a life to lead. Take me, for example:

- Full-time work.

- I have a young child.

- I have repaired my house.

- I always enjoy visiting my friends and family.

This does not leave much room for trade. I like to spend about an hour checking my cards every day, but a few days have passed. I don't want to trade and I don't want to add anything to my agenda. Some days you just don't want to trade.

Also, take a vacation. At the beginning of the year, I spent a week on Maui to recharge my batteries. In fact, I brought my cellphone, PDA, laptop and three novels thinking I was sitting on the beach or balcony taking a Mai Tai and working. In fact, I opened my computer every other day and didn't do much else. The cellphone was still connected, but for me, it's a big step forward as well. I haven't changed. I didn't see the news. I took a break and came back with a much better perspective of my company and my life. If you take the time to exit the market and finish trading, you will be ahead of the game. If you take the rest you need, we are always on the right track.

How long do you need to use a demo account before you start?

This is a difficult question and it is up to you. It depends on the type of strategy you implement. Remember to play with a demo account while developing your strategy. If you have a clear idea of what and when you will operate and what your expectations are, your trading demo should appear fairly quickly. If your expectations are irrelevant, there will be problems with a demonstration.

The other reason you may have problems with a demo account is if you do not have a clear path defined. You can simply choose random transactions in many different charts. If you do this, you are not familiar with your partner and will not learn more about their specifics. In fact, it makes trading more difficult than necessary.

Once you can earn consistent gains in your demo account that are the same as what you expect, then, and only then, you must switch to a real account. There is no urgency to change. Anyone who tells you differently has an agenda. The market has been listening for years and will continue to be. Take your time and make the right decision for you.

How is a demo different from a real account?

The best and only answer to this question is Y-O-U. Once you've got real money in the market, the game really changes. Even if it's a $ 250 mini account and you trade a lot of .01 (which I recommend), your outlook will change when real money is at stake. For whatever reason, your gains will delight you and your losses will be devastating. You will find that you are risking your losses (leaving returns instead of withdrawing as you should) and that you are assured of profits.

I would advise making a conscious effort to be brutal with your losses and take a little more freedom with your profits. As the pair moves in your direction, why not even increase your stop loss, but let it run longer if you have the moment? Define a final stop if your broker offers one, or you can manually move your stop loss as the pair moves in your direction. Wouldn't you like to get 30 pips in a 50 pips move instead of 20 pips? Don't be greedy and don't say, "No, I'd rather have 50." No one buys it at the lowest price and sells it at the highest price.

Check the passages and the relative names

It's an interesting trend. Currency pairs often move in parallel with each other, both in the same direction and exactly the opposite. EUR/USD and USD/CHF are examples of pairs who tend to have a strong negative correlation. An example of a pair with a strong positive correlation is GBP/JPY and EUR/JPY.

Check the charts and find another pair that has a close relationship with the pair you have chosen. These can serve as an early indicator or confirmation depending on the peer relationship.

Don't forget that these trends do not hold water all the time. Keep it in correlation with your other indicators. There is a well-known strategy that uses pairs who have a reverse relationship, one of whom earns a considerable amount in return, the other who pays a smaller amount in exchange.

The theory is that the transactions will cover each other and the merchant will win the exchange. Although this is an interesting strategy and many of them have success stories, keep in mind that I have also seen this strategy lose big customers. Don't be too confident and don't take advantage of everything; it's not really covered.

The graphs on the following pages show the currency pairs they have correlation and inverse relationships.

Currency pairs that tend to have a correlation relationship:

EUR/USD and GBP/USD

USD/CHF and USD/JPY

EUR/USD and NZD/USD

AUD/USD and GBP/USD

AUD/USD and EUR/USD

Currency pairs that tend to have an inverse relationship:

EUR/USD and USD/CHF

GBP/USD and USD/JPY

GBP/USD and USD/CHF

AUD/USD and USD/CAD

AUD/USD and USD/JPY

COMMON FOREX CHANGE ERRORS AND AVOID HOW

What are the most common forex errors by traders? This article will talk about all the major mistakes that traders usually make in forex markets. From the most current to the most common, this article will give you an overview of all the important things to keep in mind and avoid when you start trading in forex (or even for professional forex traders who have not yet known it).

All the people who join the ranks of financial traders, with the exception of forex, do so with the intention of making money, but only a few end up being truly profitable in forex. What prevents so many businesses from succeeding? What is different in the few trades? Currency errors can be clear and straightforward.

In fact, in an area where traders are trying to make money, a small mistake can be costly. Like any other type of trading, forex trading also requires guidance and principles to follow. Interestingly, errors in forex can be easily avoided if you can recognize them first.

The most common mistakes made during currency trading.

Lack of education

The first and foremost mistake of a beginner in forex is not a complete understanding of how markets work. Forex beginners often think that you just need to have a good trading strategy. However, they almost always end up losing money. It's almost the same as trying to start a business in an industry you don't know. Sound familiar?

Dealing with this issue is quite obvious in terms of the solution and there is a lot of discussion. Studying as if there was no tomorrow, getting a good forex education is incredibly important! Beginners have a tendency to read only a few good trading books and only a few articles before they start trading. They practice very little, forgetting they're starting a profession that takes years to master!

In fact, novice traders have so little knowledge of financial commerce that they often don't know where to start. So, how can operators avoid making the most obvious and most serious business mistake of all?

Whether studying, reading, watching webinars, attending trading seminars, practicing on a demo account, it doesn't matter. If you don't have time, take your time! You never know who the eureka moment is, nor how much you need to get a constant return.

WHAT IS A TRADING PLAN?

A business plan is a set of strict rules, half of which are guided by the business strategy and the other half by the money management strategy.

Here's how I look at it:

- Specific market conditions for entering a business

- The amount of money to risk in a business

- Specific market conditions to find out if you were wrong (stop-loss)

- Specific market conditions to determine if you are right (prevent)

- Approximate time for the market to achieve its goal

- Write and save everything

Decrease in money management

Things can get very fast in forex trading because forex brokers are very free to take advantage of their trading account, while novice traders are lagging behind in the discipline of money management. A combination of these two factors leads to high risk and high-risk trading.

Here are some points a trader should ask themselves to avoid making this currency trading mistake:

Do I invest only my venture capital? (Can I afford to lose this money?)

What is the maximum% of my total investment that I am willing to risk in an operation?

What is the maximum number of operations I can open simultaneously?

What is the profit/loss ratio promised by my strategy?

Does this respect my risk/return ratio for transactions?

Money management can sometimes become complicated because it depends on the strategy. In some cases, a strategy that promises a potential loss of $ 1,000 and a potential profit of $ 500 works eight times out of 10. While other times, a strategy that promises a $ 500 loss with a $ 1,000 profit is better, but it works five times. Trial and error is, therefore, an important part of the process and another reason why operators should use demo accounts before using their strategies in live markets.

Still, if you are new to the game or looking for new ideas, FREE trading webinars are the best place to learn from professional trading experts. Get step-by-step guidance on how to use the best strategies and indicators and receive expert advice on the latest developments in the housing markets.

Define the wrong goals

What is the wisest approach to trade? Do you do well, even if it means potentially making less profit or doing things in some way, as long as it promises more profit? This is a difficult question because what matters most to the merchant and the balance of his account is no longer about money. If the trader's sole purpose is to make money, especially at the beginning of his career, stalking money could soon become the reason for failure.

Raising money generally leads to breaking the rules of your business plan. In some specific operations, non-compliance with these rules can lead to greater returns. However, in the long run, which is your financial operations plan, it always results in a stable balance. This can happen in one of the following ways or through a combination of these: replacement and overanalysis.

Overtrading: one of the mistakes many Forex traders can come from is insufficient capitalization, forcing a trader to use large volumes simply too large compared to their account balance, or a dependency on the trading order to open.

Currency trading generally comes from highly leveraged accounts. Not having enough money to manage only increases the likelihood of a disaster. It has already been mentioned in the money management section that an operator must always decide in advance how much he will be willing to risk for transactions.

What are other traders doing? How are they used 100% or 50%? Or even 10% of your account balance in one transaction? The answer is none of them. Instead, 1% or 2% is the absolute ceiling that can be reached. How much of your capital can be involved at the same time? And with all the trades combined? The answer is 5-

7%. Such careful financial management will allow you to make room for the forex mistakes you will inevitably have, however simple as part of your learning process.

Well, how much is enough? Here is an example:

If you trade 0.01 (1,000 units of currency), which is the minimum volume of forex trading a broker can offer, you will need at least a thousand dollars of investment in an account with a slight 1: 100. It allows you to open only one item at a time. For this position, you can't set a stop loss above 50 or 60 pips, since it would make your total: 5-7%.

We are talking about a stop-fix loss, not a mind, because as soon as the price goes through a mind, an operator begins to rationalize their decisions, moving away from their initial fixed trading plan. Tip: never deviate from the business plan!

So, how can traders avoid sub-capitalization without breaking the venture capital rule? The answer: save money! You can do it. Warren Buffett saved up to about $ 10,000 during his college years by doing a variety of low-paying jobs. It looks perfect, even without the luxury of a slight 1: 100!

Problem number two – Trading unit:

Negotiating financial markets, especially in the short term, can be a very exciting activity. The markets are moving; the flow of money is real: a truly past experience. It's almost as if the market wanted to be traded. However, this illusion should not dictate your business. Do you have a plan to follow?

The hunt for money is devastating. If one seeks to increase their profits, a merchant changes his strategy, enters where he must be patient, and leaves where he must be calm. Excessive analysis goes along with the update.

Perhaps one of the biggest mistakes made by forex traders is that they think they have control of the market. They don't. Successful trading is very similar to fishing, where the fisherman has no control over the fish. You can't do much until the fish has caught your bait. Once this is done, take action. Once the market price is exactly where you want it, trade it. But before that moment, all you can do is sit down.

Your strategy tells you exactly what market conditions you should expect. Not because he lost them, or because he needs to check them in shorter terms, or because there is a gap in his strategy. The sooner you think about waiting for a market to be well-created, to start saving money instead of losing it, the better.

Objective confusion

This may seem a bit surprising to some and to many innovative traders, but financial markets are business, while most deal with entertainment or hobby. One of the major forex mistakes to avoid is to confuse the reason why you want to participate in trading. First, it influences the level of your commitment to trade.

Second, define your attitude towards the money you invest.

Entertainment is for fun. The deal is to make money. In financial commerce, invest money to make your investment profitable, which essentially makes the concept of trading an activity. If you ever hope to make money constantly in Forex trading, act as a trader.

Being too greedy

One of the common mistakes in forex trading that you can make is falling into the trap of becoming too greedy. Many forex traders have the wrong impression that they can earn 20% or more in terms of performance in a single year. Unfortunately, this is a wild hunt. Realistically, you cannot expect high returns if you are not a leading operator with a lot of experience and a good business background. Establishing the right trading goals can help you avoid mistakes in currency trading and can help you become a professional forex trader.

Minor risk management

The risks and benefits are the same in all markets. The truth is that forex beginners don't give much thought to this. Risk management is an essential element that will determine your success in trading operations. You cannot think of making a profit by blindly following a business strategy or by using only a consultant or an automated business solution. When you effectively manage your risks, getting benefits becomes a reality and not a mere possibility.

Just raise the capital you can afford to lose, and nothing more.

Believe it or not, there are many forex beginners who trade with capital that they cannot afford to lose. This can be disastrous, since forex markets, like most other markets, such as stock or fixed income, carry a risk. There is no guarantee that you will always make money. Trade losses are an integral part of trading operations.

There is also additional pressure when trading money that you cannot afford to lose. This leads you to make unfair business decisions, so try to avoid this if possible.

Ignore the psychological aspect of trade

Another error for traders is to ignore the psychological aspect that plays a role in trading. Psychology plays an important role in avoiding mistakes in forex trading. After all, markets are mainly made up of traders like you. Understanding the psychology of the market and yourself is a good starting point to recognize this error. You may now know that fear and greed are two of the most common psychological emotions that can affect your business.

To avoid this, you must not only train your mind but also approach the market.

BUSINESS ERROR

Traders without a trading plan tend to take a random approach because there is no consistency in strategy. Business strategies have predefined guidelines and approaches for each business. This prevents traders from making irrational decisions because of adverse moves. It is essential to engage in a business strategy because moving away can make traders fall into unknown territory in terms of business style. This end leads to business errors due to a lack of knowledge. Business strategies should be tested in a demo account. Once operators feel comfortable and understand the strategy, it can be translated into a real account.

Deleveraging EN

Marge/Levier refers to the use of borrowed money to open currency positions. Even though this feature requires less personal capital per transaction, the possibility of a larger loss is real. The use of leverage amplifies earning losses, so it is essential to manage this leverage.

Couriers play an important role in protecting their clients. Many agents offer an unnecessarily high level of leverage, such as 1000: 1, exposing new and expert operators to significant risk. Regulated brokers will limit their debt to the appropriate levels, guided by the respected financial authorities. This should be taken into account when choosing a suitable agent.

TIME HORIZON

Investment over time meets the business strategy implemented. Each business approach is aligned with different time horizons. Therefore, understanding the strategy will allow you to evaluate the estimated time used for transactions. For example, a retailer will indicate shorter times, while traders will favor longer positions. Explore currency exchange strategies for different time horizons.

MINIMUM RESEARCH

Forex traders have to invest in appropriate research to use and execute a specific trading strategy. Market research, as it should be, will shed light on market trends, point(s) of sale, and fundamental influences. The more time you spend on the market, the greater your understanding of the product itself. In the currency market, there are subtle nuances between the different pairs and their functioning. These differences require careful examination to succeed in the market of choice.

Avoid reacting to media and unfounded advice without verifying the strategy and analysis used. This is a common phenomenon among traders. This does not mean that these tips and press releases should not be considered, but should be systematically investigated before acting on the information.

Emotion-based commerce

Emotional exchanges often lead to irrational and fruitless exchanges. Operators often explain additional positions after losing operations to offset previous losses. These businesses generally do not benefit from any educational, technical, or fundamental support. There are negotiation plans to avoid this type of negotiation, so the plan needs to be followed carefully.

INCONSTANT COMMERCIAL RATES

The weight of transactions is crucial for any business strategy. Many traders trade sizes that are not suited to the size of their account. It increases the risk and potentially unlocks account balances. DailyFX suggests risking a maximum of 2% of the total account size. For instance, if the account contains $ 10,000, a maximum risk of $ 200 per transaction is suggested. If operators comply with this general rule, excessive account pressure will be eliminated. The inherent risk of exporting the account to a particular market is extremely dangerous.

TRADING IN MANY MARKETS

Trading in a few markets allows traders to gain the experience needed to dominate these markets without scratching the surface of a few markets. Many riot operators are turning to many unsuccessful markets for lack of understanding. This is something that needs to be done in a demo account if needed. Noise trading (irrational trading) often leads traders to make transactions without proper fundamental/technical justification in a variety of markets. For example, Bitcoins fashion in 2018 has attracted a lot of rumors at the wrong time. Unfortunately, many operators have registered in FOMO or Euphoria stages of the market cycle, which has resulted in significant losses.

NO BUSINESS MAGAZINE

Frequent use of a trading record will allow operators to identify potential strategic gaps, as well as facets of success. This improves the general understanding of market traders and their strategy for the future. The transaction review highlights not only mistakes but also beneficial aspects, which need to be constantly reinforced.

SELECTION OF A PROPER BROKER

There are many CFD brokers in the world, so picking the right one can be difficult. Financial stability and proper regulation are essential before opening an account with a broker. This information must be available on the broker's website. Many brokers are regulated in countries with weak lines to avoid narrower jurisdictions, such as the United States (Commodity Exchange Act) and the United Kingdom (FCA).

Security is the main goal; However, a comfortable platform and ease of execution are also essential to choosing a broker. There is adequate time to get used to the platform and costs before negotiating with live funds.

"I can't think and plan to do it."

Everyone knows that it is quite difficult to do anything without planning it. It is impossible to negotiate without a plan.

A business plan is a set of rules that includes your business strategy and your money management strategy. A plan will help you decide when to enter into a transaction, how to get out of a failed transaction, how much you need to take on your goal, and how much money to earn. Without this knowledge, you will certainly lose.

2. It has NO stop-loss

Even if you are 100% sure of your profit goals, you should better define a stop-loss. The forex market is very volatile and urgent news that can lead to a business change. In January 2015, the Swiss National Bank suddenly reduced the CHF limit against the euro, and the EUR/CHF parity fell by 30%. This event took everyone by surprise. Many traders who did not receive stop-loss orders suffered heavy losses. If you do not have a stop-toss, you may miss the moment of change that will lead to a disaster.

3. Get on a not-for-profit business

Sometimes, traders are so sure of their business goals that they are blind to reality. Imagine you opened a purchase order, but the market is down. However, you are so sure you have made the right decision as the size of his position grows in the hope that the price will fall back quickly. In a situation like this, it's enough to multiply the losses. If you have an open position, you lose the ability to judge impartially, and your actions become chaotic. As a result, never add a lost operation.

The same applies when an operator increases the stop-loss during a non-profit transaction so that the transaction does not end with a loss. Otherwise, your loss may be greater. If that was a bad decision, analyze what went wrong after closing the transaction, learn the lessons of this transaction, and use that knowledge to improve the trade next time.

4. Absence of risk management.

Traders who do not manage their risks can lose everything. Traders cannot afford to think only of profits. Always keep in mind how much money you risk losing per transaction per day. If you limit your potential losses, you can stay in the market for a long time and take advantage of many other possibilities. Follow the rule: 1% transaction risk. Nothing should distract you from this rule.

5. Ignore press releases

All traders know that certain events and releases are affecting the forex market. If true economic indicators differ from expected levels, currency pairs will become highly volatile. As a result, all operators, including those who choose not to exchange information, must take the information into account. Disregarding the news is a significant mistake that can be easily avoided if you plan your transactions and check the economic calendar.

6. Related pairs

Traders often try to accept trades for several days, but many do not consider currency correlations. It may seem like you have a good chance of winning with multiple pairs but beware: if you see a similar exchange pattern to multiple pairs, they are likely to correlate. This means you can win or lose at the same time. For example, USD/CHF and USD/JPY have a considerable direct correlation: when the first partner, the second is likely to strengthen as well. Then, when you buy both pairs at the same time, you double the risk.

7. Try to vindicate

Losses are difficult for everyone, especially for beginners, so it is trying to get revenge on the market. In general, sales transactions are 2 to 3 times larger than previous losing transactions. As a result, they lose even more. Loss is inevitable. Focus your energy not on revenge trading, but on analyzing failed trading and improving it in the future.

8. Lack of education

Lack of education leads to blindness and loss of business. If you want to have profitable exchanges, you must always improve your skills. If your goal is to be a terrific businessman, read educational books, discover new indicators, and practice new strategies.

THE IMPORTANCE OF SELF-DISCIPLINE IN FOREX TRADING

Patience and discipline in forex trading

Countless traders enter the forex market every day, but many fail. Some operators are too focused on creating a perfect business strategy, which leaves them little energy to develop a proper discipline. This approach is the recipe for failure because it is far more important to have a business plan that you can execute rather than a perfect plan.

If you do not have an executable strategy, we recommend learning through live trading webinars. Some traders fail because they do not give due diligence to risk management. Finally, some traders quit too soon and gave up when their strategies did not produce the desired results immediately. No tactic will generate returns every time, and operators should consider this.

Forex Trading Discipline Rules

The discipline of forex trading involves:

Develop a successful business strategy

Modifying as needed

Execute the plan effectively.

Following your plan is an essential part of the bargaining discipline. An excellent example of this importance is Jesse

Livermore, a man who "TIME" once described as "the most fabulous living merchant in the United States." Livermore made a fortune following the rules created, raising at least $ 100 million at the peak of his 1929 career.

However, Livermore decided to break his rules, causing him to lose everything more than once. To not find a similar destination, traders can follow simple rules. Three main rules, in particular, are crucial to getting a basic understanding of the discipline of forex trading. Once you feel comfortable following these rules, you can begin trading in a real account.

Business plan elements

A business plan is the basis of a merchant's success. There are many ways to create a business plan, but the crucial elements include:

- A list of trading instruments.

- What signals will you get into the positions?

- What signals will your exit make?

- Minimum duration of your exchange

- Maximum duration of your exchange

- The maximum number of transactions per day, week, and month.

Hours during which I trade.

By listing the rules below, you can not only develop your plan but also cultivate the forex discipline. Be sure to write down every market analysis done on your plan to see if this analysis fits the plan. Determine some key variables before negotiating. These variables may include the business tools you use, the input and output signals you use, and the frequency with which you trade.

After a while, you may be tempted to relax a bit. Remember, there are many stories of traders who have not followed their systems and who have experienced catastrophic results. Nick Leeson, one of those stories, was called an "original merchant." Leeson, in turn, led Barings Bank (an 18th-century financial institution based in the United Kingdom) into bankruptcy.

The bank had used it only as a major operator and even allowed it to complete its own transactions. These latter responsibilities are usually shared between different people, but Leeson was armed with both. When his speculative bets were unsuccessful, Leeson threatened his losses in an error account. These losses exceeded £ 800 million in 1995.

Why do you have to stop loss?

Most disciplined forex traders use a stop loss. Before you open the position, you need to know exactly where your stop loss will be. Once you have defined this, you should never lower it to maintain an open position. Remember, the more transactions you make, the more situations you will find in which you think your losing position will be profitable.

Some businesses find it difficult to accept losses, which can lead to bigger bets and potentially bigger losses. For example, in 2012, the principal investment office of JPMorgan Chase & Co. resulted in a loss of at least $ 6.2 billion related to derivative transactions. Bruno Iksil led the office's position in establishing complex positions involving credit derivatives, placing larger transactions in response to losses.

These positions have increased so much that some investors have said that they distort credit rates. In the midst of this interruption, Iksil received the nickname "Whale of London." Although you probably won't risk finding yourself in such a situation, this illustrates the benefit of having a stop loss to automatically close a position.

Defining a stop loss eliminates the emotions of the situation. However, while setting a specific price, and respect is an integral part of using loss control, you must take a different approach to define profit points. If it is new, it is a good idea to set a profit point for each transaction and then abstain from the change.

With more experience, you can start changing your profit points, especially if you have also started to put an end to your profit loss. But no matter if you are a beginner or a veteran businessman, you must always know your profitability before participating in an exchange.

Hours of work

The tables in relation to the financial instruments presented in this article are indicative. They do not constitute trading advice or requests to buy or sell financial instruments provided by Admiralty Markets (CFDs, ETFs, Shares). Past performance does not affect future performance.

Another important aspect of patient development and the discipline of exchange operations is to create and maintain an operations plan. If your strategy involves transactions in the opening of London markets, it will not operate at closing. But why is it necessary? You may not be aware of movements in other economies that can cause a loss in your business without planning.

In addition to setting trading hours, you need to determine the number of transactions you can make during a day, week, or month. This frequency is usually based on the type of business style you use. The latter is due to the fact that intraday operators are generally limited to a specific day, while average operators for the moment create limits for a weekly or monthly period.

Forex patience

We have covered discipline, and then we have patience. Although the two are similar, there are some important differences. Most online forex traders are sometimes tempted to prematurely conclude profit transactions, either to take profits or to avoid losing trades. To overcome this inclination, you must be patient.

Let's take a few specific steps to help you achieve this goal. First, don't let it be controlled by your fear. Having made an exchange, very few things remain that make your decision questionable. Every time you enter into a business, you need to know the maximum loss you will have, and it will allow you to earn the least profit.

Market fluctuations are perfectly normal and should not change the way you do business. Adhering to this recommended practice can take your trading at forex to a higher level. For example, MetaTrader 4 is the most commonly used trading platform in the world, despite its steep learning curve. Successful operators take the time and patience to become familiar with the tools that make winning operations possible.

Another crucial aspect of patience is to evaluate your winning transactions. As your position approaches the profit level, you may want to close it and recover profits immediately. If you follow this approach, you will quickly gain; this could also prevent your transaction from generating a higher potential profit. For example, instead of closing that position, you can choose to set your end loss to the accepted minimum profit and then change your profit by taking where the trend line is waiting. Don't forget: you can do it more than once for each job.

Discipline equals success

Long-term accounts need tighter discipline. The key is to know when to trade and when to avoid it. Typically, smaller accounts require greater risks and more operations, while larger accounts require lower risks and fewer operations. They are always making extra efforts to provide accessible fact analysis.

The purpose of these analyzes is to provide excellent business opportunities. Over time, you will learn more about price action. Regardless of whether you negotiate systems or prices, you will benefit from price action. All you have to do is follow the tripod of a successful operation: it won't be long before you start seeing positive results.

Change what you see

The beauty of trading operations is in the fact that there are many trading opportunities, so you will never feel unsure of the settings. We think you have trouble finding good positions or key trades. Still, keep in mind that you can only switch to operating in small series at a specific time of day.

Add it

Now that you've learned how to cultivate the discipline and patience in forex trading, it's time to put that knowledge into practice. Start analyzing the market and developing a business plan for your first week.

Determine from the beginning:

- What trading tools to use

- Signs that will invite your inputs and outputs.

- Your level of stop-loss profit

- The maximum number of transactions you want to perform during a given period.

Then you can apply your knowledge through a business account. If you don't have one, why not open a real account with Admiralty Markets? Or maybe practice first in a secure business environment to sign up for a demo account.

HOW TO TRADE FOREX

Traders use different strategies and techniques to determine the best entry and exit points and the best time to buy and sell currencies. Analysts and market traders are constantly innovating and improving their strategies to develop new analytical methods to understand the movement of the currency market. Here are some of the most basic categories and types of strategies developed that businesses often use.

Fundamental Analysis

In the fundamental analysis, traders will look at the fundamentals of an economy to try to understand if a currency is undervalued or overvalued and how its value is likely to change relative to another currency. Fundamental analysis can be extremely complex and complicate many elements of a country's economic data that may indicate future trends in trade and investment.

However, a good starting point for businessmen is to analyze the income and output of an economy, which is often published by the country's central bank. In addition, they can rely on news and data spread by a country to get an idea of future monetary trends.

Fundamental analysis

Whenever you hear about fundamental analysis in the forex market, you will often have a lot of information on how to do your own fundamental analysis.

Most traders (including me) end up with questions like, "I don't understand, is there a PE ration from Japan?" Well, more or less. Fundamental analysis is different for the forex market, but there are some basic principles.

A fundamental analysis of the currency market instead examines the macroeconomic indicators, asset markets, and political considerations of a country's currency. Macroeconomic indicators include growth rates (gross domestic product), interest rates, inflation, unemployment, money supply, currency reserves, and productivity. Other macroeconomic indicators include the CPI, a measure of the cost of living, and the COGS, a measure of the cost of producing goods. The asset markets are composed of stocks, bonds, and real estate. Political matters influence the level of confidence in a nation's government, the sense of stability, and the level of certainty.

Under a basic rule, a currency can become more valuable in two ways: when the amount of money available on the world market is reduced (for example, when the US government raises interest rates and reduces spending) or as demand for that particular currency increases. But there are also many small things that can increase the value of the currency sufficiently for the forex retailer to gain (or lose) a substantial amount.

Let's take a moment to analyze some of the key information that the forex market can change.

Get a panoramic view

If you want to have a solid view of the economy on the basis of the currency pair you trade, it is helpful to get a good overview of both currencies. A way to make a more fundamental summary of a currency pair is to fill in the following information:

- Daily interval (x last days)

- Weekly interval (x last weeks)

For each list of pairs:

- 52 weeks high/low

- Next meeting of the central bank

- GDP (annual growth)

- Short term interest rate forecasts

- How are inflation rates?

- Unemployment rate

Completing this form can help you examine the health of your choice.

Currency pair

Macro controls

The interest rate is an interesting figure to consider when checking the macroeconomics of a country. Be careful not to make premature decisions, as interest rates function as a divided personality and can have a strengthening and weakening effect on your currency.

On the negative side, investors often sell their business when interest rates rise because they believe that higher interest rates will negatively affect stock market prices. This can lead to a slowdown in the stock market and the national economy. However, high-interest rates tend to attract foreign investment, strengthening local currency.

Another thing to consider is the balance of international trade. A trade balance with a deficit (more imports than exports) is usually a bad sign. The disadvantages mean that money comes from the country to buy goods manufactured abroad, which can have a depreciating effect on the currency.

It is important to remember that markets generally determine whether a trade deficit is bad news or not. If the country regularly operates with a deficit, it is likely to be taken into account in the currency price. Trade deficits generally affect only one currency if it is said to be above market consensus.

Axis markets

Asset markets have an interesting link with the value of a country's currency. For example, in the past, the US dollar was moving with the stock markets. In fact, everywhere, people praise the praise of this relationship. However, if you look at the graphs, you will find that it is not really true. For some time, if stock markets are growing, the US dollar is generally declining. This may be due to the fact that American companies have more and more influence outside the United States. You can also see the same kind of influence between the Japanese yen and Nikkei.

Still, some currencies are more closely aligned with commodity prices. The four major currencies that are generally cited in relation to commodity prices are the Australian dollar, the New Zealand dollar, the Canadian dollar, and the Swiss franc. Gold and oil, in particular, are the products that have the greatest influence on the forex market, and some have touted them as leading indicators of trading operations.

The observation of the price of gold can be very beneficial for forex traders, especially given the fact that gold tends to evolve in case of inflationary fear. If you know how your currency pair reacts to gold, you may have an interesting price movement forecaster.

For example, the United States is the world's second-largest gold producer after South Africa. Therefore, the price of gold can have a significant impact on the US dollar. However, it is important to remember that gold does not normally move toward the USD; They tend to have an inverse relationship between them.

The Australian dollar also has strong links with gold, as Australia is the third-largest exporter of gold in the world. From these facts, it is easy to understand why AUD/USD tends to follow the price of gold. The other large trade influencer in the forex market is oil.

The Canadian dollar is the currency largely influenced by the rise or fall of oil prices. If you are paying attention to USD/CAD, it is interesting to see the news regarding the oil. For example, a few months ago, the price of oil rose due to the death of a former Iraqi leader. This growth has been reflected in movements in the currency markets.

This was a classic example of the use of oil prices as an advanced indicator of forex prices.

It's about politics

Politics can play an important role in the value of a currency. Many words misunderstood by a political leader can increase or decrease the value of this coin in seconds. In general, the more volatile the policy, the more volatile the currency. The political neutrality of Switzerland and the fact that much of its foreign currency reserves are traditionally backed by gold explains why the Swiss franc has been hailed as a safe haven in times of uncertainty. This means that CHF/USD ends up having a strong positive correlation with gold prices.

TECHNICAL ANALYSIS:

Most people have heard of technical analysis. It has been around for over 100 years and has been widely used and touted by warehouse and commodity traders for decades. Many of us attend a technical analysis of the advertising sales presentation. The graphic flashes on the screen, the presenter marks perfect buying and selling signs, and at the end of the presentation, you have to buy software that will tell you exactly how to trade.

The fact is, you don't have to pay a lot of money to learn the trade. Technical analysis is not difficult or scary. Once you get the basics, you will realize that there is a lot of information to learn from your charts, and everything is free to capture. Most of us have done some technical analysis, whether we know it or not. Just look at a price chart for a rudimentary technical analysis.

However, before I begin, I want to remind you that doing a good job is a skill that requires years of practice, a little training and a lot to learn from past mistakes. They do not offer you a path of wisdom and success in the market. To use a popular analogy, there are many ways to build a home. You have to decide what kind of home is right for you.

Definition

The official definition of technical analysis is the analysis of past price data to ascertain future price movements. It is the study of prices to make better exchanges. The basis of modern technical analysis is based on the Dow theory, developed around 1900 by Charles Dow. It includes principles such as the nature of price trends, confirmation and divergence, and support and resistance. Technical analysts, or charts, use a number of tools to help identify possible operations, which I'll try to explain in some cases.

Why technical analysis works (or not)

Technical analysis uses past and present behaviors to predict future behaviors. Think of it as the weather forecast. The meteorologist reviews the current weather patterns, emergencies, and comparisons to weather conditions similar to those seen in the past. If eight of the last 10 events of this type of climate have produced rain, the person responsible for the climate can confidently predict the rain.

Technical analysis works because men are predictable. People often behave in predictable ways. They systematically repeat their behavior in similar circumstances. Technical analysis is the art and science of identifying the behavior of the crowd to reach the crowd and take advantage of their momentum. This is where the often overused phrase "Master your emotions" comes into play. You have to be sensitive to what the market is doing without succumbing to the mindset of the crowd. Technical operators work hard to avoid political discussions with analysts because they believe that all the information they need is already in the price.

However, remember not to over-analyze; each action causes a reaction. Millions of traders analyze the same graphic as you, and this leads to a very fun game that can be incredibly complex, full of lanterns, traps, and treachery. Traders can be a smart group of people.

Components of technical analysis

Charts

Most technical analysts use charts as their key tool. Charts are the heart and soul of the technical analyst's tools and come in all shapes and sizes. The most common types of graphics are curves, bars, candles, points and figures, and Renko. Each price scheme has different interpretations and uses, and each has its own preferences.

Trends

If I even hear someone say, "Trend is your friend," I probably scream. Unfortunately, it is quite adequate, and it would be wise to remember that the trend is prevailing. There are a lot of books and articles that will tell you to operate with the trend. Then we shook our heads, smiled, and thought, "Yes, I'm always going to negotiate with the trend. It's completely logical. And it seems logical when you see someone drawing another graphic."

If I like it, think: "Of course! I should be a moron idiot for not seeing the trend! So I go home and look at the table and think, Hmmm, is this an upward trend? Or maybe it's a downtrend? Will we look at the one-hour chart or the 5-minute chart? What if they are different? What low points should you use? And what about this strange ascent? Trend identification is an essential tool for the technical operator."

The problem is how to define a trend. I searched the internet and found the following trend definitions:

1. derives or general trend in a data set;

2. the general direction, up or down, in which prices are changed;

3. The address (top, bottom or side) at what price and the volume of transactions is changed in the short or long term;

4. The change in a series of data for a period of years remaining after adjusting the data to eliminate seasonal and cyclical fluctuations.

It seems to me that the definition of a trend is a bit vague. Even after defining the trend, what kind of trend are you talking about? Is it an important trend, a secular trend, a micro trend? For the purpose of common sense, define a trend as a series of ups or downs over a given period, or the direction in which the price moves. But the graphics don't always move along a nice smooth line in one direction or the other. In fact, I've never seen a nice smooth curved line. Price charts tend to zigzag in a general trend line. Trends have three basic directions: up, down, and side. Most of the tools available in the market today have been designed for upward markets or trends that tend to fail miserably when the market decides to move laterally. Therefore, it is important to be able to control the stagnation of the market.

Trend lines

Do you know how to draw your own trend lines? Do you know the definition? A trend line is defined as a straight line that starts at the beginning of the trend and stops at the end of the trend. Clear as mud, right?

Choose the lowest one in one movement and draw a straight line that connects the two backgrounds. Congratulations, this is your first trend line! The reason you want to draw a trend line is to help identify places in your graph where the trend may change. This change is not necessarily out of order. It can mean from top to bottom, bottom to top, or any number of variations on the subject. Therefore, no conclusions will be reached if stock prices break the trend line. This could simply mean a pause in action before taking the same trend path.

Trend line drawings require practice and confidence. First, look for the broadest trend. If the map is ubiquitous, you can't easily identify a strong trend, and while you have time to wet your feet, don't go crazy. You will need two or three identifiable means. Remember, it takes at least two points to draw a line. If you only have two points, don't consider it a firm trend line.

Wait for the third bounce before deciding it's really a trend line. Having played it three times, it has a nice trend line. This should come back to his college physics class and the old saying that a moving body tends to keep moving until another force acts. The higher your price compared to your trend line, the more you may consider your trend line to be significant.

Also, be realistic about whether or not there is a trend line. Often, you will not be able to draw trend lines in your graph. Remember that a valid trend line is a line that helps you identify the direction of a price movement. After you start drawing trend lines in your chart, you can't stop. It is fascinating to see a rise in prices and to follow the trend, bouncing around like a rubber ball.

Once you feel comfortable with your trend lines, start looking for cloths. A getaway is a part of the price bar that goes into a line that you have drawn on the graph. You will want to be careful with falsehoods. Falsehoods can be particularly harmful because they can automatically assume that a leak means a change.

This is not necessarily true. But it is tempting to embark on a getaway since the first moments after a collapse is often the best time to get into the market movement. In my experience, it seems that an escape that occurs during a low volatility trend is more likely to be significant than an escape that is in a highly volatile trend.

You will experience your reactions to the price penetrations of your trend lines. Some businesses prefer to wait for candle after penetrating candle to make decisions regarding the validity of the penetration. You do not want to make an unthinkable decision and re-enter the market.

Support and resistance

Support and resistance lines are another valuable concept that all technical traders respect. Consider prices as a frontline battle between the currencies of the pair you're trading. For example, in the case of the EUR/USD, imagine the euro trading in one direction and the dollar in the other.

The real address of the prize reveals who wins the battle. Whenever the price reaches a certain level, euro traders increase the value of the euro and prevent it from falling further. This type of price action is called support because euro traders support the price.

Similar to support, a level of resistance is the point at which sellers take control of the price and prevent it from rising. Support levels indicate the price where most investors think prices will rise, and resistance levels indicate the price where most investors think prices will fall.

You can identify support and resistance lines by drawing horizontal lines

It's always a good idea to know the levels of support and resistance of the currency pair you're trading. Developing support and resistance levels is probably the most noticeable and recurring event on a price chart, and there are places where you want to place the potential for a profit or loss. The penetration of these levels of support and resistance leads to the formation of new levels of support and resistance. The longer the price remains at the level of support or resistance, the more this level becomes significant.

Resistance becomes support and vice versa.

When a level of resistance is successfully penetrated, that level generally becomes a new level of support. Similarly, when a level of support fails, that level generally becomes a new level of resistance.

Indicators

An indicator is a mathematical calculation applied to the price of a security. The result is a value that is plotted on a graph and used to anticipate price changes. Or, in other words, lines and graphs that you can draw on your price charts to help you understand what's happening.

There are literally thousands of indicators, and many books on different indicators are published. I won't go into all the different indicators here, but I would advise you to keep things simple.

There are four basic types of indicators: those that measure speed, momentum, volatility, and volume. Volume is not maintained in the forex market, as there is no central trading system to measure volume, but the choice of an indicator of the remaining three categories should give you a balanced view of what is happening. Check your charts. Your indicators should be the focus of your observation and graphical analysis.

Everyone has their favorite pointers. I have seen many people sell their indicators for a lot of money. My opinion is that with a little perseverance, you can find almost all the indicators you need on the Internet. Therefore, if you are ready to work, you can find what you are looking for without spending much money. Remember that most "new and fabulous" indicators are really normal indicators with some changed parameters in which someone has changed their name to ask for more sales. Do a better job and understand what your graphs are trying to say.

Convergence and divergence

You will often hear these two terms when you listen to market analysts. Convergence refers to two approaching indicator lines and a divergence with two approaching indicator lines. Convergence most often appears in price table indicators, which usually means that the price action starts to flow or has a lower range.

Reference levels

The benchmarks refer to the highs and lows in a price table. These indicators cannot be applied to a graph but can be used to indicate future price developments. When a price reaches a new historical or negative record and then returns, it may take some time before the index is exceeded. Historical levels can cause strange indicator behavior. If an uptrend indicator is mysteriously smoothed, extend the period on your chart to see if the price is close to a historical level. The market is testing these historical levels. If the test fails, you can expect a reversal and possibly a turnaround.

Adverse effects

Admitting that no one can predict a reaction has prevented many people from trying. The following lines are useful but not statistically correct, so proceed with caution.

• A rebuke will generally not exceed a high level rather than a high or low.

• Look at the round numbers. Traders are human beings, and, as individuals, we tend to like beautiful round figures. Think about it; failure in 1.2527 or 1.2530?

• 30% rule: you can assume that most operators will stop losing more than a certain percentage, such as 30%. The only problem with this is that they don't know where most traders come to market.

W.D. Gann, a renowned technician, said the best return was a 50% discount. This is the best place to reintegrate an existing trend. If the trend recovers, it will go beyond the previous peak, which identifies an immediate minimum profit target.

Fibonacci

Fibonacci numbers are named after Leonardo di Pisa, also known as Fibonacci, although they were first described in India. The best-known Fibonacci numbers are a simple series of numbers that form a sequence. After two initial values, zero and one, each number is the sum of the two previous numbers. Fibonacci numbers are studied in the context of number theory and have applications of counting mathematical objects such as sets, permutations, and sequences. Fibonacci levels are usually placed on charts to predict possible levels of recoil.

Ralph Nelson Elliot, a market expert, said Fibonacci figures can also be found in human behavior and can be mapped to predict future behavior. Elliott noted that stock market prices seemed like a wave on charts, hence the name Elliott Waves. Elliott wave members often use Fibonacci levels, with special attention to levels 38% and 62%, to predict the extent of recoil.

HOW TO TRADE FOREX USING THE CANDLE STICKS

What is a candlestick?

Japanese candles are formed with the opening, height, and end of the chosen period.

If the shutter is above the opening, we can say that the candle is bullish, which means that the market has been raised during this period. Bullish candles are always presented as a white candle. Most commercial platforms use the color white to refer to bullish candles. But no matter the color, you can use the color you prefer.

Most important is the opening price and the closing price.

- If the door is below the opening, we can say that the candle is bearish, indicating that the market has fallen during this session.

Gold candles are always presented as black candles. But this is not a rule.

You can find different colors used to differentiate the bullish and bearish candles.

- The entire part of the candle is called a real body.

- Fine lines that grow above and below the body are called shadows.

- The upper part of the upper shadow is the upper part

- The bottom of the lower shade is the background.

Size of candle body:

Candles have different body sizes. Long bodies refer to strong buying or selling pressure. If there is a candle whose fence is larger than the opening with a long body, it means that buyers are stronger and are controlling the market in this period.

On the other hand, if there is a bearish candle in which the opening is above the fence with a long body, it means that the sales pressure controls the market during the chosen period.

- Small bodies indicate a small buying or selling activity.

Shadow Sponge (tail)

The upper and lower shadows provide important information about the trading session.

- The upper shades mean the high session

- Lower today means lower sessions

Candles with long shadows show that transactions went well after opening and closing.

Japanese candlesticks with short shadows indicate that most business operations were limited to open and close.

- If a candle has a wider upper shadow and a lower shadow.

This means that buyers are flexible, and the price offered is increased. But for one reason or another, sellers have come down and lowered the price to end the session near its opening price.

- If a Japanese candle has a lower and lower long shadow.

It means the sellers have shown off their value and forced the price down. But for some reason, another buyer is coming, and prices will increase until the end of the session, close to the opening price.

Candle patterns

Candle designs are one of the most powerful business concepts. They are simple, easy to identify, and very profitable. One study confirmed that candle patterns have a high predictive value and can produce positive results.

Personally, I have been trading a sailing model for over 20 years; I really haven't changed in any other method because I've tried thousands of strategies and methods of trading with no results.

You will not be presented with a Holy Grail, this trading system works, but be prepared to lose some operations, as this is part of this game. If you are looking for a 100% win system, I highly recommend it.

Candle models are the language of the market, imagine that you are in a foreign country and do not speak the language. How can you live if you can't even say a word? It is the same when it comes to negotiation. If you know how to read candle patterns the right way, you can understand what these patterns tell you about market dynamics and business behavior. This skill will help you get in and out of the market in the right direction.

In other words, it will allow you to act differently in the market and earn money by following the trail of the smart man. The candle patterns that I will show you here are the most important models you will find in the market.

What I want you to do is focus on the anatomy of the model and the psychology behind it, as this will help you gain the ability to easily identify any model you find on the market and understand what will be required of you to do.

The model of a candlestick

The envelope bar, as it says in its title, is formed when the preceding candle is completely wrapped. The scroll bar can swallow more than one previous candle, but since it is considered a bar, at least one candle must be completely consumed. Bearish diving is one of the most important candles.

This candle model consists of two bodies: the first body is smaller than the second, i.e., the second body hangs the previous one. This is how a bearish envelope bar template appears in your graphics. This candle model gives us valuable information about bulls and bears in the market.

In the case of a bearish bar, this trend tells us that sellers control the market. When this trend occurs at the end of growth, it indicates that buyers are being unfair to sellers, indicating a reversal of the trend.

When this price trend goes up, we can anticipate a reversal of the trend, as buyers are not controlling the market yet, and sellers are trying to break the market. You can't trade any bearish candle pattern you find on your card. You need other technical tools to confirm your data.

Bearish candle patterns:

The bullish model is a bullish bar composed of two candles; the first is the small body, and the second is the candle involved.

The bullish structure of the limiting bars tells us that the market is no longer under the control of sellers and that buyers are taking control.

When an upward candle is formed in the context of an uptrend, this indicates a continuation mark. When a bullish candle is formed that includes everything at the end of a downtrend, the reversal is much more powerful since it represents a capitulation fund.

When the market changes direction after the formation of a bullish envelope bar model, the smaller agency representing the sales power was covered by the second agency representing the purchasing power. Body color is not important. The important thing is that the smallest one is totally wrapped by the second candle.

What I want to do now is get the ability to identify bearish and bullish bars in your charts. This is the most important step for the moment.

Doji Candle Pattern

Doji is one of the most important models of candlesticks. When this candlestick is formed, it tells us that the market opens and closes at the same price, which means that there is equality and indecision between buyers and sellers. When the opening price is the same as the closing price, this signal means that the market has not yet decided which direction to take. When this trend occurs in an uptrend or in a downturn, this indicates that the market is likely to reverse.

The formation of the Doji chandelier indicates that buyers cannot keep prices higher, and sellers return them at the opening price.

This clearly indicates that a trend reversal is likely to occur. Always remember that a Doji indicates equality and indecision in the market. You often find it during periods of rest after significantly higher or lower movements. When you are at the bottom or top of a trend, it is considered a sign that a previous trend is losing strength. So, if you are already following this trend, it is time to make a profit, it can also serve as an input signal if combined with another technical analysis.

Doji's dragonfly template

The Doji dragonfly is a model of a bullish candle that is formed when the high opening and closing are the same or at the same price. The Doji dragonfly features the long, low tail that shows the resistance of buyers and their attempt to raise the market. The formation of the Doji dragonfly with long and low tail shows that there is strong buying pressure in the region. If you can identify this candle pattern on your card, it will help you visually visualize where the support and demand are. When presented in a drop, it is interpreted as a bullish reversal signal. But as I always say, you can't trade a single candle pattern, other indicators and tools will be needed to determine the Doji signals of the high-probability dragonflies on the market.

The Doji grave

Doji's Tomb is the bearish version of the Doji dragonfly. It is formed when the opening and closing are identical or at the same price. What distinguishes Doji from the grave of the Doji dragonfly is the long high tail. The formation of the upper long tail indicates that the market is proving a strong production or resistance area.

Later in the day, sellers flooded the market, lowering prices. This is interpreted as a sign that the bulls are losing momentum and that the market is ready for a change. The formation of this candle pattern indicates that buyers no longer control the market. For the model to be reliable, it must be close to a resistance level.

In business, additional information will be needed on the positioning and context of the Doji tomb to interpret the sign effectively. But here, the Doji candle indicated that the vendors are struggling to break the market. The third bullish spark indicates that buyers have taken control of sellers and that the market should reverse. This is how professional operators analyze the market for candle models and analyze the financial markets if the anatomy of candle models and the psychology of their formations are dominant.

The model of the evening star

The evening star model is considered a declining investment model that is usually on top of an uptrend.

The model consists of three candles:

-The first candle is a bullish candle

-The second candle is a small candle, it can be bullish or bearish, or it can be a Doji or any other candle.

-The third candle is a big bearish candle. Overall, the evening star.

The model is the bearish version of the morning star model.

The first part of a star in the afternoon is a bullish candle; This means that bulls always push the market higher. Now, everything is fine. Smaller body training shows that buyers are still in control, but not as powerful as they were.

The third downward candle indicates that the buyer's domain is finished, and a downtrend reversal is possible. When the market was growing, the first candle of the model indicates a long upward movement. The second is a short candle indicating the consolidation of price and indecision. In other words, the trend that created the first long bullish candle is on the decline. The last candle opened the previous candle, indicating a confirmation of the reversal and the beginning of a new downward trend.

The hammer

The hammer chandelier is created when the highest price between opening and closing is approximately the same price; it is also characterized by a long, low shadow that indicates a bullish rejection of buyers and their intention to push the market upward.

The hammer is an inverted sail model when located at the bottom of a downtrend. This candle is formed when sellers lower the market after opening, but they are rejected by buyers, and the market crashes higher than the lowest price.

The hammer (bar) was a significant investment model. The long shadow represents the strong buying pressure from this point.

Sellers have tried to push the market, but at the level, buying power was more powerful than sales pressure, which caused a change in trend.

The most important thing to understand is the psychology behind this model. If you can understand how and why it was created, you can predict the direction of the market with great accuracy.

Shotgun formation is formed when the low aperture and lock have about the same price; this candle is characterized by a small body and a long upper shadow. This is the bearish version of the hammer. Professional technicians say that the shadow should be twice the actual body. The psychology behind this trend is that buyers are trying to push the market but have been rejected by sales pressure. When this candle forms near a resistance level, this should be considered a high probability configuration. The formation of this motif indicates the end of the upward movement and the beginning of a new decline. This sail model can be used with support and resistance, demand and demand spaces, and with technical indicators.

The shooting star is very easy to identify and very profitable. This is one of the most powerful signs I use to enter the market. I will tell you in detail, and show you, step by step, how to make money from this price action model.

The Harami model (the inner bar)

The Harami model (Japanese) is considered an investment and continuation pattern and is composed of two candles. For the Harami model to be valid, the second candle must be closed from the previous one.

This candle is considered a bearish reverse signal when it is at the peak of an uptrend and is an upward signal when it is at the bottom of a downtrend. When the smallest body is completely covered by the previous mother candle, do not worry about the colors, the most important thing is that the smaller body is closed to the first larger candle.

The Harami candle tells us that the market is in a period of indecision. In other words, the market is consolidating. So buyers and sellers don't know how to do it, and no one has control of the market.

When this candle pattern occurs during an uptrend or downtrend, it is interpreted as a continuation pattern that offers a good opportunity to join the trend. So, if you are at the top of an uptrend or at the bottom of a downtrend, this is considered a trend reversal signal.

Harami formation, the first upward trend in Harami, has happened at the bottom of a decline; sellers have pushed the market, prices have begun to consolidate, indicating that sales power is no longer under market control. Bearish Harami is the opposite of ascension; this happened in the upper part of an upward trend indicating that the buyer domain is over, and the beginning of a downward trend is possible. When this model is created during an uptrend or downtrend, it indicates a continuation with the direction of the market.

The latest and worst of the tweezers

The upper pair of tweezers is considered a downward inversion pattern observed at the peak of an uptrend, and the formation of the underside of the clamp is interpreted as a bullish inversion pattern observed at the bottom of a downtrend.

The upper form of the tweezers consists of two candles: the first is a bullish candle followed by a bearish candle. And the base of the clamp also consists of two candlesticks. The first candle is bearish, followed by a bullish candle. So we can say that the bottom of the forceps is the bullish version of the tweezers above.

The upside is that there is an upward trend when buyers raise prices, which gives the impression that the market is still growing, but sellers have surprised buyers by lowering the market and closing the opening of the bullish candle. This price action model indicates a bullish reversal, and we can change it if we combine this sign with other technical tools. The lower part of the clamps happens during a downtrend. When sellers lower the market, we feel all is well, but the price of the next session closes above or at the same price as the first.

A bearish candle indicates that buyers are betting on the direction of the market. If this price action comes close to a support level, this indicates that a bearish change is likely to occur.

When a bite base is in a downtrend, the bearish market has put the first downward session; however, the second session opened when prices closed in the first session and increased directly, indicating a buy signal investment that you can trade if you have other items that confirm your purchase decision.

Don't focus on the name of a candle; try to understand the psychology behind your training; this is the most important thing. Because if you can understand why it was formed, you will understand what has happened in the market and can easily predict future price developments.

CONCLUSION

The best operators develop their skills through practice and discipline. They also do a self-analysis to see what motivates their businesses and learn to keep fear and greed out of the equation. These are the skills that every trader must practice.

Currency trading can be an excellent way to diversify a broader portfolio or to leverage specific monetary strategies. Experienced beginners and marketers should keep in mind that practice, knowledge, and discipline are essential to moving forward.

Defines goals and style of negotiation

Before traveling, it is essential to know your destination and know how to get there. Therefore, it is imperative to have a clear purpose in mind and then ensure that your negotiation method can succeed. Each trading style has a different risk profile, which requires a certain attitude and a successful business approach.

For example, if you cannot sleep with an open market position, you may consider daily trading. On the other hand, if you have funds that you believe will benefit from the appreciation of an operation over a period of a few months, you are more likely to be a position trader. Just make sure your personality matches the style of negotiation you're committed to. Insufficient personality causes stress and some losses.

The broker and trading platform

The choice of a trusted broker is of the utmost importance and will be very useful for spending time looking for differences between brokers. You need to know the policies of each broker and how they create a market. For example, trading in the retail or spot market is different from trading in the publicly traded markets.

Also, make sure your broker trading platform is suitable for the analysis you want to execute. For example, if you want to compromise Fibonacci numbers, make sure that the runner's platform can draw Fibonacci lines. A good runner with a mediocre platform, or a good platform with a mediocre runner, can be a problem. Make sure you get the best of both.

A consistent methodology

Before entering a market as a trader, you need to have an idea of how you can make the decisions you need to execute your transactions. You need to know the information that will make you make the right decision to enter or leave a business. Some people choose to examine the underlying fundamentals of the economy, as well as a graph to determine the best time to execute the transaction. Others use only technical analysis.

Whatever methodology you choose, be consistent, and make sure your methodology is adaptive. Your system must contain the changing dynamics of the market.

Determine the entry and exit points

Many operators are confused by conflicting information that happens when graphs are viewed at different time periods. What looks like the buying opportunity in a weekly chart could actually appear as a sales signal on an intraday chart. Therefore, if you take your basic business address from a weekly chart and use a daily chart to get in on time, be sure to synchronize the two. In other words, if the weekly card gives you a buy sign, wait for the daily card to confirm a purchase sign too. Keep your sync in sync.

Calculate your expectations

Hope is the formula you use to determine the reliability of your system. You need to go back in time and measure all your win/lose trades, then determine the profitability of your winning trades versus the loss of your losing trades.

Check your last 10 exchanges. If you haven't done any real trading yet, return to your card to indicate where your system would indicate that you should enter and exit. Determine if you made profits or losses. Total your winning transactions and divide the answer by the number of winning transactions you have made.

Concentration and small losses

After you've funded your account, the most important thing to remember is that your money is at stake, so your money shouldn't be needed to cover your living expenses. Think of your business money as vacation money. After the holidays are over, your money is spent. Have the same attitude towards trade. This will prepare us psychologically to accept small losses, which is essential to managing your risk. By focusing on your transactions and accepting small losses instead of constantly counting your actions, you get much more success.

Positive feedback loops

A positive feedback cycle is created as a result of a well-executed exchange according to your plan. When you plan a trade and execute it well, you create a positive feedback model. Success generates success, which builds trust, especially if trade is profitable. Even if you suffer a small loss but do so according to the intended operation, it will create a positive feedback cycle.

Perform a weekend scan

During the weekend, when the markets are closed, study the weekly charts to find patterns or information that may affect your transaction. Maybe a model is a double roof, and experts and news suggest a market investment. It is a kind of reflexivity where the motive could encourage experts, which then reinforces it. In the cold light of objectivity, you will make your plans better. Wait for your adjustments and learn to be patient.

Keep a printed file

A printed file is an excellent learning tool. Print a graph and list all the reasons for the exchange, including the basics that influence your decisions. Mark the card with your entry and exit points. Make all relevant comments in the graphic, including emotional reasons for acting. Did you panic? Were they too greedy? Am I full of anxiety? Only when you can objectify your business, will you develop mental control and discipline to execute according to your system instead of your habits or emotions.